Discussing Design

*Improving Communication and
Collaboration Through Critique*

Adam Connor and Aaron Irizarry

 Beijing · Cambridge · Farnham · Köln · Sebastopol · Tokyo

Discussing Design
by Adam Connor and Aaron Irizarry

Published by O'Reilly Media, Inc.,
1005 Gravenstein Highway North, Sebastopol, CA 95472.

O'Reilly books may be purchased for educational, business, or sales promotional use. Online editions are also available for most titles (*https://www.safaribooksonline.com/*). For more information, contact our corporate/institutional sales department: (800) 998-9938 or *corporate@oreilly.com*.

Acquisitions Editor: Mary Treseler	**Cover Designer:** Ellie Volckhausen
Development Editor: Angela Rufino	**Interior Designers:** Ron Bilodeau and
Production Editor: Kara Ebrahim	Monica Kamsvaag
Copyeditor: Dianne Russell	**Illustrator:** Adam Connor
Proofreader: Kim Cofer	**Compositor:** Kara Ebrahim
Indexer: Ron Strauss	

June 2015: First Edition.

Revision History for the First Edition:

 2015-06-09   First release

See *http://www.oreilly.com/catalog/errata.csp?isbn=0636920033561* for release details.

ISBN: 978-1-4919-0240-0

[LSI]

[contents]

[*Foreword*]

Critique requires an investment.

This investment certainly comes from the person who provides the critique; he has an obligation upon accepting the request to provide you with an ability to act and/or react to his input. (There is a bit of beauty here in that you get to decide how to act and/or react to his input, and that can be to do nothing with it. You should, of course, be prepared to explain why you did nothing with it.)

Your investment (and your responsibility), however, is much, much greater. It is you who are obligated to set up your audience to provide you the critique that you want and need through a structured request. It is you who needs to provide people a proper context—the scope and goals for the critique—to set the proper expectations and to frame the critique that allow you to explore possible improvements.

This might sound simple enough; however, the reality is that most people don't operate under any formal rules of critique. Instead, a lot of times designs are shared over email, through project management software or other design-sharing services, in chat, or through other rather narrow communication channels. Reactions and responses turn up in Reply All bullet points, fragments of disjointed and combined discussion threads, and even worse, piecemeal over a period of time.

Indeed, hell can be other people.

In many cases, we're to blame.

Designers have to not only respond and react, they also have to try to organize and coordinate discussions, thoughts, and debates and then try to iterate. And then, the process is repeated again (and sometimes again, and again) as a new draft is sent around again, bereft of context or explanation of what's been updated.

This is time consuming and fraught with potential mistakes and out-of-scope requests. And, for the love of all things holy, think of the timelines and budgets!

Unfortunately, this really isn't uncommon. It's possible that you were just nodding your head in agreement while you were reading that, thinking of that one project that was such a tremendous pain at that one employer where the client, the boss, and everyone else were so impossible to work with. I get it. I've been there in the thick of that trap, and I've perpetuated it, too.

It doesn't have to be any of these ways, and picking up this book is your first step toward ensuring that those vicious cycles stop happening around—or worse, because of—you. The most successful designers know that good, structured critique guides them through the design process and helps them to produce their best work. They know that they bear the burden of ensuring they get what they need from others involved in the project in order to make a design work, and they know that this helps make it a lot easier to sell their work to their clients.

Read this book. Read every last page of its critique-detailing goodness. And then apply it to your design practice. You'll make some mistakes along the way; however, you'll also find yourself improving at critique from your very first attempt. Before you know it, you won't consider any other way to create your best work.

Adam and Aaron are two of the best designers I know, and this is largely due to their focus on unlocking the vault that holds all the secrets to good, structured critique. They're not only great designers, they're also kind and generous souls who are sharing all that they've learned with us so that we, too, can be better designers and serve our clients and our purpose as best as we can.

I've been lucky—I've been able to witness Aaron and Adam as they've gone through the exploration of critique. What started as a joint presentation turned into a website. That then turned into workshops at some of the best-known conferences around the globe, which then turned into a detailed book proposal, which finally turned into the book you're holding in your hands. I've learned so much along the way, and I've improved my own practices and approach to design critique along the way. I've been able to work with teams where we invested a very small percentage of our time in critique and in turn felt that the investment was returned incrementally. I've put their practices into use in the practice of design and also in content creation, presentations, teaching, and more.

This critique stuff works.

This book is a lot like reliving Adam and Aaron's journey for me, and it's a reminder of all the things that I can still do better through the practice of proper critique. I look forward to hearing your stories about how critique has helped change and improve all that you do, too.

—RUSS UNGER
JANUARY 2015

[*Preface*]

The Lost Skill of Critique

"Make it pop some more."

"I don't really like it... I am not sure why, but this isn't it... I'll know it when I see it."

"What the hell is this?"

"Can you make it look like Apple?"

"You should move that text to the top of the page and make all of the buttons icons."

If you have spent any time building, designing, or crafting something— or working with those who do—you have probably heard something along the lines of these statements, which are often followed by something like, "Well, I'm just giving you some feedback."

Or, perhaps you were part of a program in school that included critique where your professor tried to "break you down" for your own good. Although this is not the situation in all academic settings, some schools and educators use critique and feedback sessions as a way to prepare students for the "real world," but often they just leave students upset and with some bad memories.

There is a lot of ambiguity around feedback and why we share it with others. When feedback lacks a focus and appropriate purpose it is counterproductive and can even be harmful at times. Even in social interactions we see this type of feedback being used to express opinions. So often, when a new product is released or updated, before you know it the masses are providing 140 characters of opinion about what should have been done or created.

The more we hear stories (and experience situations ourselves) of out-of-context opinions, harsh phrases, and directional statements shared as feedback, we've seen that the real value and utility of feedback as part of design and creative processes being lost.

In short, we've forgotten how to critique. Because of this—and because of how feedback often is used—we harm not only the products and services we create, but our teams, organizations, and working relationships, as well.

Critique is supposed to be helpful. It should be an analysis that helps us understand what is working and what isn't and whether we are on the right track toward reaching our goals. But the critique and feedback we see in so many teams doesn't do this. Instead it's often used as a way for individuals to assert their own authority or push their own perspectives and objectives. It could be someone trying show expertise to others in the room by pointing out all of a design's faults without the real intention to help the design get better. I have also seen individuals pick a design apart as a way to eliminate any competition between the design being reviewed and their design.

The practice of real critique has become a lost skill.

The lines have become blurred in relation to feedback, critique, and how we communicate while working together. So the questions arise. What can we do to better understand the issues that are keeping us from productively talking about what we are designing and ensuring that it meets the goals that were set for it? How can we improve the way in which we give and receive critique so that it is helpful?

What This Book Is About

This books sets out to answer these questions in a way that provides individuals, teams, and organizations with techniques, tools, and resources that will help them improve the quality and usefulness of the conversations surrounding ideas and designs within their teams and with their clients.

We will analyze and define critique and examine the good, the bad, and the ugly of both giving and receiving it. We'll examine the cultural aspects that support or hinder critique. And, we will provide tips and insights on how to integrate critique as a part of your process.

Why We Wrote This Book

This book was born from many conversations that Adam and I were having separately with our peers on the topics of feedback and how we would like to see it improve in our practices and community. A mutual friend, Whitney Hess, gave us the idea to collaborate on this content together. Before long a blog post turned into a conference submission, which in turn grew into many talks and workshops at conferences and for companies across the United States.

The more we heard individuals' stories and were asked about how this content could be worked into various teams and environments it became clear that putting together a book that could be used both as an examination of critique and communication as well as a reference for advice and tips would prove helpful.

That is the core of why we wrote this book. We have been there. We have heard the harsh feedback and tried to work with a lack of useful comments and "suggestions." We have felt the nervousness of presenting designs to teams and clients for feedback and we have had our designs shredded and picked apart, leaving us feeling defeated.

We have also felt the satisfaction that comes from having productive conversations about what we are designing, feeling like you can do something actionable with the insights gathered. We wrote this book to help teams better communicate about what they are designing together, to improve collaboration, and establish a framework for productive critiques.

Who Should Read This Book

Maybe you're thinking, "That's all well and good, but I'm not a designer or artist. Why should I read this book?"

To that, we'd look you dead in the eye and say something like, "Designers and artists don't own critique. Critique is for anyone who wants to improve anything that they are building or doing. Critique isn't a 'design' skill, it's a life skill."

This book has been written based on experiences that included multiple roles within teams and organizations: product owners, project managers, designers, developers, executives, marketing professionals, and more. If you are a part of a team or project working to design or create something, you are a part of the conversation surrounding it. This book serves as a reference for anyone who is a part of the process and can help team members work to improve how they communicate and collaborate with one another.

Terms We Use

Though we have written this book for anyone who is a part of building something, we are using some general terms throughout the book for the sake of consistency.

We will use *designer* to refer to anyone who has come up with an idea or works on the creation of an idea in any way.

We will use the term *product* to refer to whatever it is that is being created or is being proposed.

Critique and *feedback* are often seen as interchangeable terms, and to some extent they are; we will explore common misunderstandings of these terms and how they work together best.

How This Book Is Organized

This book will cover the various aspects of critique, its definition, and how we interact with one another in critique settings.

Chapter 1: Understanding Critique

In Chapter 1, we explain the various forms of feedback that are often seen in a critique setting, the challenges that come from specific forms of feedback, and the types of feedback we should look to gather. We will also discuss the various perceptions associated with critique.

Chapter 2: What Critique Looks Like

In the second chapter, we talk about what critique looks like and the importance of intent in the critique process. We also cover best practices for giving and receiving critique and tips on how to know when you are not giving good critique.

Chapter 3: Culture and Critique

Chapter 3 explores aspects of our individual and organizational cultures that influence our ability to effectively critique. We also look at some of the common barriers that you can encounter when trying to establish a productive critique practice.

In addition, we discuss the foundational elements that teams can use to effectively critique any effort, such as goals, principles, and scenarios.

Chapter 4: Making Critique a Part of Your Process

In Chapter 4, we talk through making critique a part of your process, and some of the challenges that come with this effort. We will cover things to remember when making critique a part of your process. We will also cover the areas where we see critique taking place (standalone critiques, design reviews, and collaborative activities) and their differences. Chapter 4 also covers when, how much, and how often we should critique.

Chapter 5: Facilitating Critique

Facilitation plays a key role in critique. In Chapter 5, we dive into this skill and how to use it to keep critiques effective and on track.

We share rules that you can use to help participants understand how a critique session is supposed to run and what to avoid doing to help make the session productive.

Chapter 5 also covers how to prepare for, kick off, run, and follow up after a critique. It includes tips on who to include as participants, advice for presenting designs, and making sure everyone understands not only the goals of the product but the goals of the critique session.

Chapter 6: Critiquing with Difficult People and in Challenging Situations

It's inevitable that as you work to improve collaboration, communication, and critique, you'll encounter situations and individuals that present a challenge. In Chapter 6, we examine some common challenging situations and strategies we can use to work through them.

We'll also discuss what to do when people become difficult in a critique, providing tips and techniques for dealing with them and still salvaging the critique. If you've ever experienced someone giving you a list of changes or a design showing what they want instead of feedback, we explain how to respond and get back on a path to critique.

We hope that the breakout of these chapters will not only provide a solid understanding of critique as you read through it, but that they are broken out in such a way that they can be used as a reference when needed.

Chapter 7: Summary: Critique Is At The Core Of Great Collaboration

We circle back around and summarize main points from each chapter, putting a nice bow on everything and preparing you to get out there and improve the design conversations you have with your teams.

Acknowledgments

Aaron—I would like to thank my amazing and beautiful wife, Amanda Marie, and my daughters Ashlyn and Audrey who are the inspiration for all I do. Adam Connor, you are my partner in rhyme, and I consider myself immensely fortunate to have been able to collaborate with you on this content; your friendship means even more to me. To all of my luchas at the Daq, it is truly an honor to work with you.

Adam—To my wife, Tria, and my kids Owen and Lily: thank you for being my energy and inspiration and for supporting me and putting up with all my excitement and stress during the course of writing this book.

To my parents, Kerry and Martha, and my sister, Meghan: thank you for always believing in me through all the choices I've made and things I've set out to do.

To Aaron: it's been awesome, my friend, and turned into far more than I ever thought it would during that first Skype call. Thanks for being there every step of the way and for your collaboration and friendship.

To my Mad*Pow family, especially Amy Cueva, Mike Hawley, and Dan Berlin: thank you for always having my back and pushing me too keep going.

To my MassMutual family, Jenny Fabrizi, Dawn Vitale, and Donna Hiersche: thank you for believing in me and helping me see that I can take my ideas as far as I want to.

From both of us—To Mary, Angela, Sonia, Nick, Marsee, and everyone at O'Reilly: you are amazing to work with. Thank you for your patience and guidance.

To Whitney Hess: thank you for getting annoyed enough with each of us after so much bitching about this topic and suggesting that we start bitching together. Who'd have thought that it would start such an interesting journey?

To Russ Unger: thank you for your kind words and contributions to this book. Your friendship and guidance are more appreciated than you know.

To Jared Spool: thank you for seeing something in our vision and message and for helping us hone and share it with so many people.

To our amazing friends and contributors, Kim, Jeff, Brad, Kevin, Chris, and Veronica: it is a great honor to have your thoughts and stories in this book, thank you.

And to all our friends...

Angel Anderson	Debra Gelman	Will Sansbury
Stephen Anderson	Megan and Matt Grocki	Bill Scott
Chris Avore	Andrew Hinton	Boon Sheridan
Fred Beecher	Shay Howe	Amy Silvers
Scott Berkun	Phillip Hunter	Ian Smile
Dan Brown	Jessica Ivins	Brad Smith
Michael Carvin	Leslie Jensen-Inman	Carl Smith
Carolyn Chandler	Jennifer Jones	Joe Sokohl
Dana Chisnell	Joel Kilby	Kyle Soucy
Denise Chroninger Philipsen	Jonathan "Yoni" Knoll	Joan Vermette
Adam Churchill	Donna Lichaw	Todd Zaki Warfel
Josh Clark	Dave Malouf	Thomas Vander Wal
Abby Covert	Christian Manzella	Noreen Whysel
Lauren Cramer	Amy Marquez	Christina Wodtke
Christian Crumlish	Matt Nish-Lapidus	John Yuda
Jenn Downs	Eduardo Ortiz	
David Farkas	Adam Polansky	
Ian Fenn	Lynne Polischuik	
Nick Finck	Lou Rosenfeld	
David Fiorito	Dan Saffer	
Aaron Gustafson	Ant Sanders	

...and to everyone who has supported our talks, workshops, and this idea as a whole over the years, you have our utmost gratitude!

Understanding Critique

Conversations Matter

Whether you're a developer, project manager, designer, business analyst, and so on, it's more than likely that you've been in a meeting in which the topic of "design" has come up explicitly or otherwise. No matter what you're designing—a tool, a service, a product, a brochure, a logo, whatever it might be—you're going to be involved in conversations about how it works, what it can do, what it contains, how it looks, and more.

Collaboration and coordination are critical elements in the success of projects in most (if not all) modern organizations. There isn't a single individual who is responsible for coming up with an idea, designing it, building it, selling it, and supporting it. Instead, these responsibilities and the expertise that come with them are divided among a variety of contributors who each bring knowledge to the team. So, we need to work together, combining our skills and know-how. And to work together, we need to talk with one another. We need to discuss what it is we're designing, why we're creating it, and how it will all come together.

But as many of us have experienced, conversations about design can turn painful. At a minimum, when these discussions go wrong, they delay progress. They seem to go nowhere. People disagree, argue, and team members walk away not sure what to do next.

Although individual instances like this might not seem like a huge deal, it's the culmination of discussions that go this way that really affects a team. Over time, delays accumulate; the resulting lack of momentum and repeated questioning of what to do next gives rise to a sense that none of the team members seem to agree, which has a tremendous negative impact on people. They stop wanting to collaborate and they begin to care less and less about the project. In some cases they begin to silo themselves, feeling that because they can only control their own output, it will be their sole focus without regard to the other team members and how it effects them.

In some cases, though, these conversations can become much worse. As people talk about what they think should or should not be a part of the design, it's not uncommon for individuals to become emotional. For some, this can be difficult to control, which can lead to people getting defensive, tempers flaring, yelling, berating, and lines being crossed.

The intent of this book is to help make the conversations that happen as a part of projects more effective and productive with regard to their objectives. These discussions are always happening. Sometimes, they take place in a formal setting such as a meeting. Sometimes, they're more informal, perhaps when we're standing in line to pay for a cup of coffee. No matter where these conversations occur, we need to be able to discuss our work.

Unfortunately, we don't often take time to examine these conversations and understand what makes them good or bad. This book looks at the elements of these conversations and the patterns through which they arise. It also describes best practices for making these conversations more productive to projects and toward strengthening a team's ability to collaborate through incorporation of critique, an often-overlooked component of the design process.

The Problem with Asking for "Feedback"

Requesting feedback on a design or idea is one of the most common ways design discussions are initiated. Feedback is a common element and activity in not just our workplace cultures, but in many social cultures, as well. "Feedback" is a word that's become ingrained in our vocabulary. We use it all the time, à la "I'd love to get your feedback on something…"

During a project, a designer might just grab someone at a nearby desk because she wants to take a break from putting her design together and think about what she's done so far. Or the feedback request might be part of a planned milestone or date in the project's timeline, often called *Design Reviews*.

It's not that either of these is a bad time to get other opinions. Rather, the real problems we encounter come from the word "feedback" itself, what it means, and how we ask for it.

WHAT IS FEEDBACK?

The issue with feedback lies in how nonspecific it is. Feedback itself is nothing more than a reaction or response. Designers talk about feedback and feedback loops as an important element in design all the time. In a feedback loop, after an individual takes an action, the object or environment on or in which that action has taken place changes (or reacts). The individual then interprets that change or reaction in consideration of what they'll do next. (See Figure 1-1.)

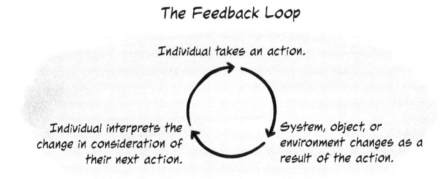

FIGURE 1-1
The three stages of a feedback loop

Figure 1-2 depicts a feedback loop designed by the team at Ready For Zero. In it, as a user manipulates the sliders or values of the various fields in the form to figure out her payment plan on a credit card, the other values all adjust instantaneously. This allows the user to see the effect that adjusting a value, like her monthly payment amount, will have on the total amount she pays and how much she might save.

Make your plan.

Enter or select a total dollar amount you can afford to pay each month or choose the date you want to be free of debt.

MONTHLY PAYMENT	$100.87
●	
DATE FINISHED	05/06/2017
●	
YOUR DEBT	$2,025.44
+ INTEREST	$405.08
= TOTAL YOU WILL PAY	$2,430.52

You will save 11 years, 9 months and $1,887.10 vs. paying minimum payments.

Make your plan.

Enter or select a total dollar amount you can afford to pay each month or choose the date you want to be free of debt.

MONTHLY PAYMENT	$151.26
●	
DATE FINISHED	08/09/2016
●	
YOUR DEBT	$2,025.44
+ INTEREST	$253.82
= TOTAL YOU WILL PAY	$2,279.26

You will save 12 years, 7 months and $2,038.37 vs. paying minimum payments.

FIGURE 1-2

Example of a feedback loop in UI design from Ready For Zero

That reaction—the noticeable change in the appearance or state of the system—is the feedback. It is the system's response to what the user has done. Feedback is a reaction that occurs as a result of the user doing something.

In human-to-human interactions such as the conversations we have in our projects, the feedback we receive might be nothing more than a gut reaction to whatever is being presented. And to be quite honest, even though we might not want to admit it, that's often all it is.

Someone's reaction tells us a bit about how he feels regarding what has happened or been designed, which can be useful in some cases, but also presents us with some challenges. Chapter 2 points out that a reaction on its own doesn't go far enough to be helpful in allowing us to improve our designs and move forward in our projects. Not only that, the reaction might be based upon the personal biases and preferences of the individual who is reacting, which might or might not align with a mindset representative of the audience for our product.

There is a popular saying in many design communities: "You are not the user." It's important to keep that in mind when we're discussing the things we're designing and deciding what should or shouldn't be a part of them. It's not that we only want feedback from users, but when collecting feedback from people in other roles we need to ensure that the user's needs, goals, and contexts are kept in mind.

The problem with asking for feedback is that, most times, we aren't being specific enough in describing what we want feedback on and why we are asking for it. Sometimes, the feedback we receive might just be a gut reaction. Sometimes, we might get back a list of instructions or suggestions on what to change. Sometimes, we might get comments that describe how what we've designed doesn't match what the critic would have designed. Weeding through all of that feedback to try to determine what's of use to us—what will help us identify the aspects of our design that we should iterate upon—can be a struggle.

Central Idea

Feedback is an important part of the design process, but the term itself and the way we often ask for it is very broad and can produce conversations that aren't useful. We can improve these conversations by understanding what feedback is and how we use it.

THREE KINDS OF FEEDBACK

There are three forms of feedback, all of which vary in their degree of usefulness to us in the design process. Understanding these three kinds of feedback can help us understand the conversations we have with our teams and improve our own ability to react to and use feedback to strengthen our designs.

The first two types of feedback

Figure 1-3 illustrates how reaction-based feedback tends to be emotional or visceral. It happens quickly and instinctively. This type of feedback is often filled with passion. It's driven by someone's personal expectations, desires, and values. Essentially, it's a gut reaction.

FIGURE 1-3
An example of reactive feedback

There is another kind of reaction-based feedback that is driven by the individual's understanding of what they are expected to say, typically driven by a cultural understanding or what they think the presenter wants to hear. In this case, the reaction itself isn't in regard to what's being presented; rather, it's in response to simply being asked for feedback in the first place. Examples of this kind of feedback often take the form of "That's wonderful! Great work!" or "I love what you did with…"

Why it can be an issue
At best, this kind of feedback informs us about the subconscious reaction the viewer has to what you've designed. These kinds of reactions are something we do want to understand when designing a product or service. It's not ideal to try to sell something potential customers or users cringe at or grumble about the second they see it. But are the people from whom you've asked for feedback reflective of your design's actual audience? Are they looking at it the same way your potential users would? Does this reaction divulge anything specific about any of the design decisions you've made so far or their effectiveness?

Direction

Direction-based feedback, as seen in Figure 1-4, typically begins with an instruction or suggestion. In many cases that's also where it ends. In this form of feedback, the individual providing it is often looking for ways to bring the design more in line with their own expectations of what the solution should be. You might also have encountered examples of this kind of feedback that start with phrasing similar to, "If I were to do this..." or "I would have..." or "I wish..."

FIGURE 1-4
An example of directive feedback

In all of these, the individual giving the feedback is trying to communicate her own vision for the design. It might be because she has her own detailed solution already in mind, or it might be that she feels a problem is not being adequately solved. In some cases, the individual will go on to describe why she is making the suggestion, which can shed a bit more light on her thinking and motives.

Why it can be an issue

Similar to reaction-based feedback, direction-based feedback without any explanation indicates nothing about the effectiveness of your decisions in meeting the design's objectives. Sure, if the person giving you feedback is the one who will ultimately approve the design, she might supply you with a to-do list that you could act upon to get her approval, but getting that approval and creating an effective design are not necessarily the same things.

For situations in which the individual also gives some explanation as to why she is making the suggestion, you at least begin to understand the impetus and perhaps the issue she's trying to address with it. But, it still does not help you understand how or why the design you have is or is not effective at addressing that problem.

Additionally, when left unchecked, this type of feedback leads to problem solving which, although an important part of the design process, is counterproductive to the conversation you're trying to have. It's not that the direction itself that is being given is a bad idea, but at this point it's out of place. We look further into problem solving and its impact in Chapter 5.

How to deal with reactive and directive feedback will be examined further in Chapters 5 and 6. For now, what's most important is to understand what these forms lack in terms of their usefulness in helping us to improve our designs.

WHAT WE REALLY NEED IS CRITICAL THINKING

Critical thinking is the process of taking a statement and determining if it is true or false. When we're designing something, we're doing so to meet or achieve some set of objectives. When looking for feedback on our designs, we should be working to understand whether we believe that what has been designed will work to achieve those objectives. We should be looking for a form of analysis to take place. And that's exactly what critique is.

Critique: The third form of feedback

It's this form of feedback that is most helpful to us in understanding the impact of our design decisions.

Good critique is comprised of three key elements:

- It identifies a specific aspect of the idea or a decision in the design being analyzed.

- It relates that aspect or decision to an objective or best practice.

- It describes how and why the aspect or decision work to support or not support the objective or best practice.

FIGURE 1-5
An example of critique

Let's look at Figure 1-5 and examine its parts to see how they align with these three elements:

- *If the objective is for users to seriously consider the impact to their bank balance before making a purchase...* This states the objective the person giving the feedback is analyzing.

- *...placing the balance at the bottom of the screen at the same size as all the other numbers...* This segment identifies the design choices made that are being analyzed.

- *...isn't effective because it gets lost in all of the other information.* This part tells the designer that the critic does not believe the choices he made will be effective and why.

Critique isn't about that instant reaction we might feel when seeing something, or about how we would change someone's design to better solve an issue. Critique is a form of analysis that uses critical thinking to determine whether a design is expected to achieve its desired objectives (and adhere to any pertinent best practices or heuristics).

Those objectives can be any number of types of things. They can be about utility, for example giving someone the ability to complete a task. They can be about metrics and measurement, as in increasing the number of conversions for a particular call to action. Or, they can be experiential, for example making someone feel excited or surprised by something.

Chapter 3 provides more details about the role of these objectives in design projects and in setting the foundation for productive conversations, but hopefully this begins to give you a sense of how critique differs from other forms of feedback.

Knowing what we want and what we're asking for makes all the difference in how our conversations play out. It might seem like little more than semantics, and it's damned difficult to give up using the word "feedback" when asking to talk with people about an idea or design (in fact, we'll be using it over and over again in this book). But, as you'll see as you read the coming chapters, what's important is to understand the differences in forms of feedback and to use that understanding to inform how you ask people and facilitate the resulting conversations.

Central Idea

Feedback encompasses three forms: reaction, direction, and critique. Reaction and direction are limited in their ability to help us understand if the design choices we've made might work toward the product's objectives. Critique, a form of analysis that uses critical thinking, is feedback that focuses on exactly that understanding.

CRITIQUING SOLO

This book centers on critique as a form of conversation we have with our teams. But it's important to note that an individual can and should also critique alone, analyzing his own work.

When designing something, the brain operates as a toggle, switching between creative thinking—where individuals are generating ideas or assembling parts of ideas—and analytical thinking—where they are determining whether what they've designed so far is in line with what they are trying to achieve. Experienced designers, artists, engineers, and others have learned how to be deliberate in controlling when to make this toggle, periodically pausing their creative work to take a step back and critique what they have so far.

Why Critique Is So Important

Throughout this book we'll dive deeper into the various ways critique fits into the design process, but as we get started, it's important to identify these patterns and benefits in order to keep in mind the broader application of the concept.

CRITIQUE BUILDS SHARED VOCABULARIES

Have you ever noticed how as people spend more and more time together they begin to talk like one another? They begin to use the same phrasing of words and names for things. This is a natural occurrence in social groupings—it's part of a process called acculturation.

Intuitively, we seek out efficiency in communication with others. Communication between individuals grew out of the need of one individual to produce action by another. It isn't very effective if we need to spend all of our time getting our point across. As we build a shared understanding of what words and phrases mean among a group, we instinctively begin to use them over other words that might mean the same thing. By avoiding words that aren't as easily recognized by the others in the group, we streamline and improve the quality of our conversations.

One challenge project teams face in collaboration is the variety of language used by people in different roles. Members from IT, design, and business might all have different ways of referring to the same thing. By bringing your project team together to critique on a recurring basis, you provide a venue for this shared vocabulary to build up and take hold. As that vocabulary is being built, it's happening across roles and silos, improving the ability of team members to communicate more efficiently with members of other roles.

CRITIQUE AS CONSENSUS FINDER

Design-by-committee and "frankensteining" (the mashing up of design elements, features, and so on from various ideas and sources) are much-hated phenomena in the design community. Both terms are often used to imply the misguided amalgamation of ideas into a final design without any attention paid to their disharmony or whether they really work to achieve the desired outcomes.

In environments where this takes place, the driving force is typically to get those involved, particularly stakeholders, all saying yes to what is being designed without regard to whether what is being designed is actually the best solution. And so, bits and pieces are added to appease the various influencers of the project. But here's the thing: there isn't anything wrong with combining elements from different ideas to make a new one. The weakness here is the reasons why the elements being combined are selected. Critique is what's missing from the process. Selections aren't necessarily based on the elements of an idea that are most effective toward a particular objective.

In these environments, critique might still be happening, but it's typically found happening in a small corner of the project team. A few people, maybe the designers and developers, are doing it but the entire team isn't.

What Aaron and I have found in teams that carry a culture of critique is that, at any time, these discussions involve members of the team from across departments and disciplines. It becomes a natural part of the way they talk with one another. It isn't always a formal meeting or a specific request such as, "Could I get you to critique something with me?" As the project progresses and decisions are made, critique is just part of the conversation. Members are consistently focused on and discussing the elements of the design that work best to achieve its goals. Consensus begins to be found around which ideas are stronger or weaker, and the design is strengthened as a result.

> Years back, on a project that involved the creation of a new insurance application and processing platform, I got a call from one of the developers. She had been working on building out some of the functionality I had prototyped for the initial submission of an application. While doing so, she was stopped by a stakeholder who had an idea for a new piece of functionality that they were hoping could be added to the screens. A few minutes later, the developer had given me a call (I worked in another office), set up a screen-share, and she, the stakeholder, and I were discussing the new functionality and the ideas for its inclusion in the design.
>
> As we did, we referred back to the task flows and scenarios we'd created for this particular set of functionally as well as the goals we had for individuals using it. In doing so, we quickly realized that the functionality itself didn't fit the objectives we were after. It would have created an awkward branch in the task flow and more work for the user. We also saw, though, that the main point of this new functionality was to give the users (insurance agents) a view of a key piece of data that had been missing from our designs. When we realized that and agreed that being able to see that data was important to our objectives, we were able to generate a few ideas for adding the data value to the screen in an effective manner. The entire process took less than 30 minutes, and afterward, the stakeholder, developer, and I all walked away, confident that we had improved the design.
>
> **—ADAM**

In the preceding story, even though critique wasn't sought out explicitly, it was a key part of the conversation and decision-making process. This is what we mean when we talk about critique being part of a great team's natural language. Yes, the team might carve out specific times and meetings for a formal critique session, but critique also finds its way into other conversations. The team understands that in order to make good decisions about what to design and how to design it, it needs to think critically about its options and objectives.

CRITIQUE AS ITERATION DRIVER

Critique is part and parcel of an iterative process. Chapter 3 spends more time looking at iteration, but it can't be understated how closely these two are tied. If we're going to look at design as an iterative process—something that takes a creation and evolves it from idea to final product and further—there need to be points in our process that drive that evolution and indicate where changes should be made moving forward (that is, the next iteration).

Many organizations use various testing and observation methods such as usability studies and beta releases to do this today, but depending on your market and audience, these approaches can take a lot of time. Sometimes, you just need to take a quick step back. In the early stages of design, my team at Mad*Pow might iterate three or four times on a design in a single day. All we do is ensure that after sketching and developing ideas for a period of time, maybe as short as 10 to 15 minutes or as long as a few hours, we stop and examine what we have so far against our objectives and best practices. Iterations don't always have to be huge readjustments of the entire design. Sometimes, they might be much smaller and focused on a handful or even just one interaction, or flow or design element.

In these cases, the drivers of our iterations are the discussions our teams regularly go through. Most are self-induced, meaning that they're not dictated by a date in someone's project plan; rather, they can be initiated by the designer or design team when they feel like it's time to take a break from designing and look critically at what they have so far.

Central Idea

Because critique, when done well, focuses on analyzing design choices against a product's objectives, it also provides teams with additional benefits, acting as a mechanism for building shared vocabulary, finding relevant consensus, and driving effective iteration.

Critique as a Life Skill

By now, we hope that you are thinking about the processes your own organization goes through in projects. That's exactly what this book is about, but hopefully you've noticed that what we're really talking about here is something that applies beyond the boundaries of a business or organization. It applies any time and to any activity or thing you want to improve, whether it be improving a new recipe; honing your skills in Ultimate Frisbee; playing the ukulele; or painting portraits of people's pets with macaroni, hot-glue, and food coloring. Whatever it is, you can incorporate critique to help you improve upon it.

As mentioned earlier, critique is really about critical thinking. As we work toward doing or designing something with a set of objectives in mind, we always have the opportunity to stop and analyze what we've done so far to better inform how we might go forward. Critique is an act of reflection. It is part of the learning process. If Aaron and I might be so bold as to say, critique is a *life* skill, not a *design* skill.

GIVING CRITIQUE THE ATTENTION IT DESERVES

If critique is so important, why don't people pay more attention to it? Why don't teams take time to practice and talk about it?

Improving the quality of critique, or more specifically, improving a team's skills at facilitating and giving critique, should become a priority. Doing so can be tremendously valuable and can result in better collaboration, efficiency, and designs. The first steps to doing this are to overcome three myths that are often part, if not all, of the cause for critique to be overlooked.

Myth 1: Critique is a meaningless term used to make feedback sound more important

This one is pretty weak, but it's worth addressing because we've seen it come up in more than a few organizations with which we've worked.

In media today, the term "critique" has become a label used to categorize anyone's opinion on something. Media personalities, writers, pundits—anyone, really—can offer their perspective on a new product, service, or policy and call it a critique. It's come to mean nothing more than one person or group's thoughts on what another person or group has done. The aspects of critical thinking and of focusing on what the originating person or group's intentions were have gone out the window.

But we know that that isn't really what critique is about. Understanding the qualities that separate critique from other forms of feedback—and helping our teammates understand those qualities as well—results in more efficient, useful conversations.

Myth 2: We don't need to talk about or practice how we give feedback

When your team engages in a postmortem or retrospective for a project, what do you talk about? Most likely you talk about the decisions that were made, maybe a little about the process with regard to the kinds of meetings you had or when they happened. Have you ever talked about the language you use when talking to one another? Have you ever talked about how specific conversations were framed and facilitated?

When we think about our processes we tend to focus on a level higher than where the quality of critique is really influenced. Talking is something we take for granted, and so the details of how we do it are often glossed over. But there is that old cliché: the devil is in the details. Or, more accurately, it should be that the devil is in ignoring the details.

The ways we talk to one another, initiate conversations, ask questions, and so on all effect how our conversations unfold. If we really believe that those conversations are important to our team and project's success, then it stands to reason that thinking critically about them, talking about them, and practicing our techniques are important actions for improving them.

Myth 3: Critique is something only designers or other creative people do

Critique can sometimes be thrown into the "creative professional" silo as something only artists, designers, and the like do. It's not for everyone else.

What individuals and organizations that fall into this trap fail to realize is that when a project is tasked with making something, no matter what it is, every single team member is a part of the design process. Design doesn't just happen in the design department. It happens with every decision about what will or won't be part of the final product, whether that's a feature, a paragraph of content, a color pallet, a user interface pattern—anything.

If we truly want to improve our processes and improve the way our team members work together, we can't ignore the details and we can't silo our critical thinking. Yes, there are roles and responsibilities that each team member will carry based on their expertise and knowledge, but critical thinking about what we're designing is a part of every member's role.

Incorporating Critique and Moving Forward

The remainder of this book is about that role and the best practices and methods we have at our disposal for making sure it's fulfilled. As we dive deeper into the details, you'll begin to see just how pervasive critique can be, how many places it can pop up, and how many parts of your process it can help you to improve.

The ultimate goal for teams that are interested in improving conversations and collaboration with critique is not to add one more tool or type of meeting to their ever-growing toolbox. Instead, it's to change the way we talk about what we've designed regardless of the type of meeting or conversation we're in.

Critique itself is often referred to as a *soft skill*. Soft skills are often thought of as interpersonal behaviors and characteristics that influence how we interact and communicate with others. Whereas *hard skills* tend to be applicable to a specific task, action, or type of work, soft skills apply broadly across most activities and work. As we examine critique throughout the book, it's important to keep in mind two key aspects:

Critical thinking
> This is the examination of what you're designing against the objectives for its creation.

Delivery
> This is how you present your critical thinking to the others with whom you're working.

It should also be noted that critique isn't just about pictures. Often, it can be seen as a process that only applies to a wireframe or a visual design mockup or maybe a prototype, but in reality, critique can be applied to just about anything.

Any time you or your team construct something or make a decision about something in order to reach a specific goal or fulfill a certain objective, it is something that can be critiqued. For example, you're team might establish a set of design principles to help guide you in deciding between ideas for an interface. There are best practices for establishing and using design principles. A good design principle should help you eliminate more ideas than you pursue, and it should be specific and avoid overly subjective and ambiguous terms like "fun." As such, with best practices like these, when your team creates principles for your next product or project, you have an opportunity for critiquing your principles against them.

Central Idea

To ensure that our conversations with teammates are as useful as they can be, we need to think about how we apply critical thinking to the topics we discuss and how we share with others the insights we achieve as a result of that critical thinking.

Wrapping Up

Over the course of a project, team members will have countless conversations in which they collect or provide feedback on designs. Sometimes, these conversations can be unproductive, painful, or even toxic. Improving these conversations begins with understanding what critique is, how it relates to feedback, and the value it brings to our teams, projects, and products:

- Feedback has three forms: reaction, direction, and critique. Reaction and direction are limited on their own in helping us understand whether our design will work toward achieving its objectives.

- How we ask for and collect feedback has a significant effect on which forms of feedback we receive as well as its relevancy and usefulness in helping us to improve our designs.

- Critique, the third form of feedback, is analysis that uses critical thinking to ask whether what we've designed will work to achieve the established goals and objectives. It can, and should, be a part of any formal or informal discussion we have about what we're designing.

- Beyond the benefits we get from the analysis done in critique, it also helps teams to do the following:
  - Build shared vocabularies, making communication more efficient.
  - Find consensus based on product objectives when deciding between multiple design options.
  - Inform and drive iteration on aspects of a design where they are most needed.

Unfortunately, critique is often overlooked for a number of reasons, but by recognizing its value and spending a little time understanding what it is and how it fits within our teams and processes, we can improve the quality of the conversations our team members have and make critique a natural part of our communication and process.

[2]

What Critique Looks Like

The Two Sides of Critique and the Importance of Intent

There are two sides, or roles, in any critique:

Recipient

> The individual(s) receiving the critique (that is, the designer or pre-senter of whatever is being analyzed) who will take the perspectives and information raised during the critique, process it, and act upon it in some way.

Giver

> The individual(s) giving the critique—the critics—who are being asked to think critically about the design and provide their thoughts and perspectives.

Within both of these roles there is the discrete aspect of intention: why are we asking for/receiving/giving feedback? Intent initiates conversation and is often what separates successful critiques and feedback discussions from problematic ones.

For the best discussions, the intent of each participant—regardless of whether they are receiving or giving critique—needs to be appropriate. If we aren't careful, critique with the wrong or inappropriate intent on either side can lead to problems not only in our designs, but also in our ability to work with our teammates.

Receiving critique with the appropriate intent is about wanting to understand whether the elements of the design will work toward the established objectives for the product.

Giving critique with the appropriate intent is about wanting to help the designer understand the effect that elements of the design will have on the product's ability to achieve its objectives.

Both acts are done with the intention of using the information and perspectives raised during the critique to modify and strengthen the design. This is an important aspect of the discussion. Many of us have experienced meetings during which we've been asked to give our thoughts on something like a design, or a process, or maybe even a project (for example, a postmortem or retrospective). Over time, if these discussions repeatedly fail to produce action and changes, our desire to participate and provide our perspectives wanes.

Part of what makes for strong critiques is the desire to participate and to help. To be certain, everything said in a critique is not going to produce a discrete modification to the design. But overall, participants should feel that the discussion, to which they actively contributed, will play a role in improving the design—not just changing it, but strengthening its ability to produce the desired objectives.

Prior to beginning a critique, whether you're the giver or receiver, it's best to ensure that you're going in with the right intent.

Giving Critique

Giving critique with the right intent is about wanting to contribute to the improvement of the design by helping the designer understand the relative success design elements will have in working toward the stated objectives. When we approach our feedback discussions with this mindset, we think critically about what we're saying and why we're saying it. By considering both the *what* and the *why*, we keep conversations productive.

To better understand what giving a good critique looks like, let's first analyze some characteristics of bad critique. For more tips on handling and working with unhelpful feedback and unwanted critique, see Chapter 6.

THE CHARACTERISTICS OF BAD CRITIQUE

In most cases, what causes a critique to be characterized as "bad" is usually a set of behaviors or characteristics exhibited by those involved. The following subsections present a few that we have seen.

Selfish

Bad critique can sometimes be the result of selfish intention. That's not to say that it is always malicious, but it might be focused on or driven by the critic's personal goals and come at the expense of the team or other individuals, specifically the designer of whatever is being discussed.

In extreme cases, selfish critique comes from the motivation of the giver to not only be heard and attract attention, but also to be recognized as smarter or superior.

The most recognizable examples of this can be seen on social networks such as Twitter or Facebook whenever there is a change to a popular app, device, or other trend-worthy product. A new feature is added or something is changed, and people immediately begin slamming decisions, labeling them ridiculous and stupid, and stating how things "should have been designed."

But in most of these situations, the commenters have only a cursory understanding of what the designer or team was working toward and the constraints they were working within. How is this helpful?

When we do this (and Aaron and I are guilty of it, too), are we really trying to help someone improve his design? Or are we more interested in showing others in our community or organization how smart we are on a certain topic?

Selfish critique and feedback happens on project teams, as well. Maybe you've encountered it at work, are thinking of a colleague who's done it to you, or maybe you've done it yourself.

Sometimes, this kind of feedback comes from having our own ideas of what we think the design should be, but not having had a chance to share them with the team. So, we set about to use feedback as an opportunity to propose our own alternative ideas for how something could be done. Although Aaron and I are firm believers that a great idea can come from anywhere, and team members in any role should be given an opportunity to share their ideas, doing so during a critique is detrimental.

As is discussed in Chapter 5, critique is not the place for exploring new ideas. Its purpose is to analyze the design as it has been created so far. Shifting a group from an analytical mindset to an explorative one is best done with deliberate facilitation.

It's important here to recognize that not all selfish critique is malicious. Some individuals might simply be unaware of their tone, or they have difficulty forming their feedback in a way that is useful. When presented with selfish feedback, we have an opportunity, and often a responsibility, to work to understand what someone is trying to tell us and determine if it is useful in helping to improve our design.

Untimely

Despite what you might think and what some people might even say, people aren't always looking to hear feedback on their work. Unless someone has specifically told you that they would like your feedback, it's unwise to think your conversation is a great opportunity to share your analysis with her. If someone is telling people about her creation, it might just be to get the word out or simply that she's excited about the project.

For the receiver to really listen, process, and make use of critique, she needs to be in the proper mindset. Whether at a team member's desk, in a meeting, or on social channels, when critique is uninvited, it can lead to defensiveness, communication breakdowns, and often paints the person giving the critique as a "know it all."

Incomplete

For critique to be useful, the designer(s) need to understand not just the potential outcome or reaction to an element of their design, but the "why" behind it. We often see feedback in the form of things like, "I think the button is better than the link" or "Nobody is going to click that." Or, even worse, "This is terrible…"

This type of feedback typically comes from the reactive form of feedback discussed in Chapter 1. It lacks the critical thinking that makes it possible for those working on the design to understand what they might need to change in their next iteration. For these critiques to become valuable, they need to be followed by an explanation as to "why" the giver is having that reaction or foresees a certain outcome. For example, "Nobody is going to click on that because the current page design leads the eye down the left side of the screen away from the call-to-action."

Good critique is actionable. When the "why" behind the feedback is included, the designer can fully understand the comment and take action. That is to say that the designer has enough of an understanding of what is and isn't working and why it isn't working that she can explore alternatives or make other adjustments.

Be aware though that this is different from prescription or direction. Critique should not tell the designer how to act on something or specifically what changes she should make (the directive form of feedback). Good critique avoids problem solving because it can detract and distract from the analytical focus of the discussion. For more on this, check out the section "The Rules of Critique" in Chapter 5.

Preferential

Another common characteristic of bad critique is feedback that is justified by the giver from purely preferential thinking. We've all heard horror stories about this kind of feedback. Designs are torn apart not because a particular aspect isn't working toward its objective, but rather because it doesn't match exactly what the critique giver "likes." For example, a website design is discarded because the color scheme reminds a stakeholder of a Christmas sweater his ex-wife gave him.

It might seem ridiculous, but this kind of feedback is common, though maybe not always so extreme. It usually feels like it's coming out of nowhere and has no relevance to the work we're doing, but sometimes, it really just boils down to a personal preference.

This kind of feedback is not only unhelpful—it does nothing to analyze a design with regard to objectives—but it can also be distracting and counterproductive. This is especially the case when it comes from team members or stakeholders who are in a position of approval. In these situations, the team begins, consciously or subconsciously, to prioritize that individual's tastes alongside or above project and user goals, even if they conflict.

BEST PRACTICES FOR GIVING CRITIQUE

Whereas critique with the wrong intent (done knowingly or not) is harmful and can damage teams, processes, and most important the product, useful, productive critique has the ability to strengthen relationships and collaboration, improve productivity, and lead to better designs. To give the best critique possible, think about the following best practices when giving feedback.

Lead with questions

Get more information to base your feedback on and show an interest in their thinking.

Chances are, before being asked for your feedback, the presenter will give a brief explanation of what he has put together so far and how it would work. This gives you some context and understanding of the objectives he has and the elements of the design he has put in place to achieve them. But he likely hasn't explained everything. Actually, as we'll talk about later on, *hopefully* he hasn't explained everything.

This is your chance to open up the dialogue. By asking questions you give yourself more information on which to base your analysis and give stronger, actionable feedback. If done in a noninterrogative way, it shows the designer that you're genuinely interested in not only his work, but the thinking behind it, which can make discussing it and listening to feedback easier for him.

Examples of questions you might ask:

- Can you tell me more about what your objectives were for [specific aspect or element of the design]?
- What other options did you consider for [aspect/element]?
- Why did you choose this approach for [aspect/element]?
- Were there any influencers or constraints that affected your choices?

Remember though, the dual purpose of asking these questions of the designer:

- To get more information
- To make the designer more comfortable talking about his thought process and decisions

How you ask these questions can have a huge impact. Asking every question beginning with "Why..." can feel abrasive or like an attack. Use lighter, more inviting phrasing such as, "Tell me more about..."

Use a filter

Hold on to your initial reactions, investigate them, and discuss them in the proper context, as appropriate.

You're going to have reactions. As the work is being presented to you, there will be things that make you think "Huh?" or "That's cool," or "I don't get it," or maybe something worse. Hold on to those reactions and remember that they don't typically make for useful feedback. Ask yourself why you're reacting in that way. Ask the presenters additional questions if necessary to help you understand your reaction.

After you understand your reaction and what caused it, think about when it makes the most sense to discuss that reaction and to what length. Does it relate to the objectives of the product, the audience for it, or any particular best practices that should be followed? Or, is it more about your personal preference or wishes for how you'd like to have seen it designed?

If your feedback is related to the product's objectives or best practices and not about your personal reaction or preferences, it likely has a place in the conversation. Sometimes, though, you might find yourself with feedback that, although not a best practice or preference, is also not specific to a best practice or a stated objective. Maybe it's something new that you think should be considered. What should you do in those situations?

In these cases, it might still be useful to bring your feedback into the conversation. These kinds of thoughts can be useful in determining additional objectives or constraints for the project that need to be exposed. It might be something you can discuss quickly and then continue on with the critique, or it might prove to be something sizeable that needs a separate, dedicated discussion so that the critique isn't derailed.

Don't assume
Find out the thinking or constraints behind choices.

"To assume makes an ass out of you and me." Most of us have probably heard that line a few times in our lives. It's one of the favorites of Adam's father and it has stuck with him.

Making assumptions can be one of the worst things to do during a critique. When we make assumptions we begin to form our thoughts, questions, and statements around them, without ever knowing whether they're accurate. Before you know it, the participants of the discussion leave to work on their action items based on very different ideas and produce work that doesn't align with that of the other participants.

When you make assumptions in a critique about what an objective or constraint might be, or maybe that there were no constraints and the designer could have done anything, you begin to offer feedback that could be less useful because it isn't based on the real situation.

Avoiding assumptions is simple: ask about them.

Yup. Ask yet more questions. Put your assumption out there and ask if it's accurate. If it is, continue on with your insights. If it isn't, you might need to adjust your thinking a little.

For example, if your feedback is based on the assumption that the designer had no constraints and could have done anything, ask him if he faced any constraints that influenced his choices. Or perhaps ask him if he had wanted to take a different approach but couldn't due to a constraint.

Don't invite yourself
Get in touch and ask to talk about the design.

In the previous section, we noted untimely feedback as one of the types of unhelpful critique. If the recipient of the critique isn't of a mindset or isn't ready to listen to the feedback and use it, chances are she will ignore it or the critique could potentially cause a rift in your working relationship.

If you have thoughts about someone's design and she hasn't explicitly asked for your feedback or critique, get in touch with her first and let her know. Politely suggest that when she's at a point when your thoughts might be helpful, you'd be happy to share them. Give her the opportunity to prepare to listen.

Talk about strengths

Critique isn't just about what's not working.

We sometimes have a tendency to focus on negatives, the things that cause us problems, get in our way, and that we'd like to see changed. We often take the positive for granted. In our project meetings and design discussions it's often no different. We spend the vast majority of time talking about what isn't working. But that can be harmful. Remember that critique is about honest analysis. It should be balanced, focusing on the design and its objectives, regardless of their success. It's just as important to talk about what is working and why as it is to talk about what isn't working.

Often when talking about the role of "positive feedback" in critique, we see discussions center on the importance of discussing strengths as a mechanism for making critical feedback easier for the receiver to take. There is a common structure often discussed called the "OREO" or "sandwich" method in which you begin by offering a positive piece of feedback, followed by a negative one, followed by another positive one. It's a fairly common technique, and you can read more about in Chapter 6.

But there are other reasons for making sure that critiques include discussion on what aspects of the design are working toward objectives and why and how.

Part of the design process involves the deconstruction and abstraction of ideas and then recombining them in different ways or with ideas from somewhere else. It's a common way in which we take a familiar concept for which there is room for improvement or added value and then innovate from there. When we talk about aspects of a product or design that are working, there is the potential for the designer to examine those areas and abstract concepts or elements from them that could be used to strengthen other areas of the design that might not be working as well.

Additionally, with the understanding that the designer(s) will iterate upon his design after a critique, how bad would it be if at the next critique you noticed that an aspect of the design that seemed great previously had now been changed and wasn't quite as effective. And this happened because it hadn't been talked about, so the team didn't see a reason not to change it.

Think about perspective

From whose "angle" are you analyzing the design?

In the previous section, we talked about preferential critique, or feedback that's based on personal preferences rather than being tied to objectives for what we're designing. When we're analyzing a product, it can be easy to forget that we most likely aren't representative of the product's target audience. Even if we are a potential user, we know far more about it than the average user.

As you analyze a design, it's important for you to try to balance your expertise against the user's perspective. It can be difficult to achieve, but by simply asking yourself, "How am I looking at this?" when you examine an aspect of the design and comparing your perspective to what you think the user's might be, you're off to a good start. From there you might find that one is clearly more appropriate than the other (your visceral hatred of the shade of green being used probably doesn't matter), or perhaps it might be best to bring both up in the discussion. For example:

> From the user's perspective, I think all of the steps in this flow make sense and are understandable and useable. But from an interaction design perspective I think there might be some redundancy and opportunities to simplify...

Surface-Intended Fidelity and Nail Your Timing

One of my favorite collaborators is a creative director and graphic designer named Chris Cashdollar. Before you ask, yes, that *is* his real name. Chris and I worked for several years together at a web design agency called Happy Cog, where I served as the experience director. I oversaw a small team of experience design and content folks, while Chris oversaw graphic designers.

Kevin M. Hoffman, Founder, Seven Heads Design

Chris Cashdollar, Founder, Cashdollar Design

Experience design and creative direction often overlap in skillsets, process, and proclivities; in some agencies the two aren't even considered separate groups, existing simply as "design" (or "Design," if you're fancy). During our time working together, I approached design discussions by getting at the user's perspective via a solid understanding of interaction design conventions, metrics, and insights from research. Chris evaluated design based on a deep conceptual understanding of the designer's intention as it related to choices in graphic direction. Together, we were a formidable force for great design.

Our collaborative culture was informal. One of my favorite critique stories occurred during the design of the Zappos website. In looking over a designed page, it felt like it was missing an experience that captured the delightful nature of the brand. I proposed a tool that suggested shoes based on ridiculous combinations of people and occasions such as "I'm a robot going to a nightclub." It resonated well with the designer and eventually the client. That culture of openness yielded good ideas like this often, but it also lead to clashes and disagreements, especially when feedback was *both* unsolicited and unstructured. That doesn't help at all. I'll let Chris tell you what that feels like:

> Designers get a bad rap as being introverted and sensitive. In the midst of an otherwise productive design critique, I've seen them become sullen and withdrawn—or worse, defensive and angry. Collaborative discussions about improving design easily devolve into a turf war with camps entrenched in their opinions on direction without setting proper expectations.

The right feedback at the wrong time ruins momentum and causes design-ers to abandon good thinking. It also invokes stress and negativity into office relationships. Designers feel as though their shiny, new Camaro-of-a-design just got T-boned while waiting for the light to turn green. Their attention (and thus the feedback they were expecting) was elsewhere. That's why the wrong emotions kick in and, unfortunately, the work suffers.

By taking the extra time to converse with a designer prior to a critique, you'll have a common understanding of what is on the table for discussion. Are you talking about concept or art direction? How is branding applied? Create the appropriate boundaries for the critique so that all parties under-stand what specific aspect of the work is under scrutiny, and whether it's still developing or a follow-up on something finished.

Creating those boundaries is something Chris and I learned to encourage in our teams from years of working together. To prevent those misunderstand-ings and poorly timed comments, I always ask two simple questions *before* telling anyone what I think. They might seem obvious, but by asking them I respect choices that have been made so far, and I open the conversation to reach its full potential.

Where are you in your process?

This question reveals a designer's intended fidelity of thinking. Everyone's design process is different, and in many cases they vary from project to project. By understanding where a designer feels like he is in his own journey, I can tailor the language in my feedback to reflect that. Is something about to go to a client? Then, it's probably too late to revisit larger decisions. Is this early thinking? Then, don't pick on details; look for more interesting conceptual discussion. This ques-tion usually uncovers the designer's rationale for key decisions very quickly. Knowing the intended fidelity of someone's work goes a long way toward not reacting to something they may have not even consid-ered yet.

What can I help you with the most?

Gut reactions are going to be informed by experience and expertise, but they aren't going to be organized because they're shooting out of your gut instincts. Asking this question helps me to organize my reac-tions into something designed to address the designer's immediate stumbling block. Whether the feedback is solicited, asking this ques-tion gives the conversation a chance to serve a purpose. Opinions are easy. Help at the precise time it's needed is difficult, but not impossible.

Hopefully these two quick and easy questions will help you frame slower, more difficult discussions in more meaningful ways.

Central Idea

Giving good critique is a skill that begins with the right intentions. Help the recipient understand how effective the design is by making sure that you're avoiding selfish, untimely, incomplete, or preferential feedback and by following best practices.

A SIMPLE FRAMEWORK FOR CRITIQUE

It's helpful to have a sense of what the structure of a good critique sounds or looks like. As Chapter 1 instructs, critique contains three important details:

- It identifies a specific aspect of the idea or a decision in the design being analyzed.
- It relates that aspect or decision to an objective or best practice.
- It describes how and why the aspect or decision works to support or not support the objective or best practice.

To ensure that we uncover and include all of these details there is a simple framework of four questions that we can ask ourselves, or the other individuals participating in the critique, as shown in Figure 2-1.

What is the objective
of the design?

What elements of the design are
related to the objective?

Are those elements effective
in achieving the objective?

Why or why not?

FIGURE 2-1
The four questions that comprise the basic critique framework

These four questions flow together to generate feedback in the form of critique. By asking these questions, we collect the necessary information with which we can think critically about the design we're examining. Let's take a look at these questions individually.

What is the objective of the design?

We want to understand what we're analyzing the design against so that we can focus our attention on things that are pertinent to the conversation and the improvement and success of the design. Try to identify the objectives that the designer was aiming to accomplish through the choices she made. What are the objectives of the product or design that have been agreed upon by the team?

What elements of the design are related to the objective?

Next we identify the aspects and elements of the design that we believe work toward or against the objective. Whether the aspect or element is the result of a conscious choice by the designer doesn't matter. We are analyzing the effectiveness of the whole design as it's presented.

Are those elements effective in achieving the objective?

Now that we are thinking about specific objectives and the aspects of the design related to them, it's time to ask whether we think those choices will work to achieve the objective. This is the crux of critical thinking.

Why or why not?

Finally, we need to think about the result that we think the choice will actually produce. How close is it to the actual objective? Is it completely different? Does it work counter to the objective? Maybe it won't work to achieve the objective on its own, but in conjunction with other elements of the design it contributes to the objective.

Note that the first two questions can be reversed in order depending on how the design is being presented. These questions form the foundation for the critical thinking that comprises good critique. As such, these questions can be asked and answered internally by individuals giving feedback, or they can be exposed and asked directly of the designer. As mentioned in the earlier section on best practices for giving critique, it's great to lead with questions. And questions that ask about what choices were made and what objectives those choices were intended to achieve are a great way to start the conversation.

Other questions to think about

The four framework questions help us formulate feedback that a designer can use to better understand the effectiveness of his choices when viewed against his objectives. But, what about other aspects of the design? What about other questions that come up? For example:

- What new problems, complications, or successes might arise from the choices being proposed?

- What other objectives should the designer have been considering, but didn't?

Raising these kinds of questions can be important. Ignoring them might mean missing something that becomes problematic later in the project's timeline, or it might give rise to a new objective for the team to discuss and agree to (or discuss and agree isn't an objective).

With additional questions like these, however, it's important to keep in mind scope—both the scope of the product and the scope of the feedback discussion. These questions can lead to spending too much time discussing things that are outside the scope of the project or product itself, like perhaps a known issue that the product isn't intended to solve. Or, questions like these can take the focus off of the aspects of this design for which the presenter is looking for feedback, and instead use up valuable time on elements of the design that haven't been fully thought out yet and are likely to change anyway.

The group, both the recipient and the givers, need to be conscious of this potential for scope-creep and be prepared to end or defer a discussion when it begins to move out of scope.

About objectives

As we've mentioned and will continue to reference throughout the book, critique is about analyzing something against its objectives. But what exactly are these objectives? In Chapter 3 we'll describe four aspects that we feel establish the objectives of a product: personas, scenarios, goals, and principles. These elements frame a product and provide an understanding for team members of what they're trying to create.

Additionally though, when we describe objectives, we should be considering best practices—heuristics that have been established over time to help us understand how best to approach or solve for a given situation. Ignoring these in a discussion would be detrimental. As you analyze someone's work, it's likely that, if you are well versed in a certain set of heuristics, you'll identify areas of the design that are in or out of alignment with those best practices. These observations should be included in the discussion. An objective of anything we design should be to align with best practices where applicable.

Central Idea

Forming critique is a simple four-step process. What are the design's objectives? What are the elements of the design related to those objectives? Are those elements effective? Why or why not?

Receiving Critique

Listening to people comment on something you've created can be scary. It can be difficult enough to present something to a group of people, never mind the possibility that they then might begin to pick it apart.

> While I was in film school, at the end of each year we were required to present our final film to an audience of classmates, instructors, family, and friends. At the end of my first year, I presented my work, a short film that debated who was the better superhero, Batman or Superman (the answer is Batman, of course). Following the credits, I walked to the front of the room, talked for a few minutes about it and waited for the comments.
>
> I didn't have to wait long.
>
> One of the professors began to tear into it, commenting on how pointless it was, how little depth it had, how the actors didn't move enough yet were working in a medium called "movies."
>
> Those 12 minutes still haunt me. And for a very long time after that, I was terrified of showing my work—any work. On multiple occasions over the years, that fear became so significant that I threw out everything I created. Even when I moved into the business world, the

prospect of standing there and listening to feedback terrified me. And, unfortunately, I've had numerous encounters with coworkers that have reaffirmed that fear.

—ADAM

Many of you might have had similar experiences, or have heard enough horror stories that you feel like it's happened to you, too. All of this fear and trepidation can lead us to change our behaviors and expectations when presenting our work and asking for feedback.

Just like giving critique, receiving it in a way that is useful and productive requires the recipient(s) to have the right intentions. When receiving critique you should be in a mindset to step back from your creative thinking to examine the choices you've made to better understand how to proceed and take your design further. And you should value the expertise and perspectives of your teammates in doing so.

Often, though, we see individuals and teams go through the process for the wrong reasons, leading to issues down the road as the project progresses, both for the product and the team's relationships.

CRITIQUE ANTI-PATTERNS

When engaging in critique, there are patterns (or behaviors) that go against critique best practices and can hinder the critique process. The sections that follow describe these patterns.

Asking for feedback without listening

Sometimes, we ask for feedback because we feel like it's the right thing to do, or because we feel like we have to. Although stepping back and forth between creative thinking and analytical thinking is a key component of a successful design process, it isn't the case that we're always in a position mentally or tactically to listen, consider, and utilize feedback to improve our designs.

If we ask for feedback or critique, we need to be ready to listen to whatever we receive in response. Asking for critique at a time when we don't really want it or can't do something with it leads to unproductive discussions. By not listening to our teammates, we miss valuable insights that can help improve our designs. The people critiquing our work are likely to pick up on your disinterest and, as a result, will feel uninterested in sharing their thoughts. Over time, they'll be less inclined to participate in these kinds of conversations at all.

Remember the importance of being able to switch between creative and analytical thought. Getting used to making this switch between creative and analytical thinking may not always feel comfortable. But if we learn how to use it effectively, by making critiques a scheduled part of our process, it can go a long way to strengthening us and our team's skills as designers. For more on formal critiques and the design process, see Chapter 4.

Asking for feedback for praise or validation

Creating something can feel awesome. Whether we're designing alone or as part of a team, it's not unusual to want to be recognized for our creations. But it should not become our motivation for asking for feedback.

And yet we do it often. We share our work with statements such as "Hey! Check out this thing I just made! I'd love your thoughts on it," when really the only thoughts we want to hear are "Way to go! Looks awesome!" and "Congratulations!"

So we wait for the cheers. Some come, and it feels great. But then we get some feedback about things that aren't so great or things we could have done better, and it hurts. No matter how valid the points might be, we might not be in the proper mindset to hear them. Some people will become defensive. Others might argue and try to discredit the feedback. Some ignore the comments. But either way, we haven't done a very good job at receiving critique, even though you asked for it.

Not asking for feedback at all

Because you're reading this book, and you've made it this far in, hopefully you understand the value in critique and how it can help you to improve your designs and products. If that's true, then you should also see how important it is to seek out critique.

If we don't take the initiative to ask for critique or feedback in a way that helps us understand and improve upon our ideas then we'll miss a huge opportunity. We can't just assume that others will come to us with feedback. And we can't assume that just because no one comes to us that we've designed the perfect solution. By bringing others in to help us analyze our ideas we can take advantage of their experience and expertise to inform our design decisions in ways we aren't able to do on our own.

Central Idea

Ask for feedback, and when you do, be ready to listen and act on what you learn.

BEST PRACTICES FOR RECEIVING CRITIQUE

Receiving critique in a way that is productive goes beyond just asking for it and then sitting back to let others give you their thoughts. When receiving critique, keep in mind the best practices that follow.

Remember the purpose

Critique is about understanding and improvement, not judgment.

There is no such thing as a perfect solution. There is always room for improvement. A goal of a critique is to help identify where those opportunities are. The conversations we have during critique act as roadsigns along the evolution of our ideas and designs, helping us to understand which paths might take us closer to our end goals. Critique isn't about pass or fail, approval or rejection. It is a reflection used to inform a next step.

Listen and think before responding

Many of us have a bad habit of not really listening when someone is speaking to us. We hear the first few words they say, and then instead of listening to the remainder of what they're saying, we begin to formulate a response and wait for the first opportunity to start talking.

What this means is that while the person we should be paying attention to is explaining a thought, instead of listening to and processing that explanation we've essentially ignored it. It's not that we've done so maliciously; this is a common occurrence and most of us do it. Obviously though, this is counterproductive to what we're trying to do in a critique.

When receiving critique it's important that we work toward preventing any natural tendencies to form rebuttals and instead focus on listening to people's entire thoughts. This doesn't mean that as the recipient we must sit silently throughout the critique. Figure 2-2 shows that— after listening to a piece of feedback—the responses we give should be intended to ensure that we understand what the critic is trying to tell us. We can ask what the critic means. We can answer his questions. We can provide more details about how we came to the decisions in our designs if it's necessary to help the critic with his analysis.

Return to the foundation

As people share their thoughts with you, you might encounter feedback that seems out of place. It might seem as though the feedback has little to do with what you're trying to design or the objectives you have. The person you're hearing from might just be having difficulty connecting her thoughts, or it may be that she has begun to offer feedback that is based more on her own preferences or goals.

FIGURE 2-2

Demonstration of dialogue that helps ensure stronger feedback by allowing the recipient to seek clarification and ask questions in order to make sure they understand what is being said

To help you determine this, you can use previously agreed-upon objectives. A product's objectives describe the reasons for its creation, who it is for, and what it will do (more on this in Chapter 3). If you can't determine for yourself how the feedback relates to the product or project's objectives, try to work with the person giving the critique on relating it back by asking her follow-up questions related to the objectives.

If, over time, you're able to determine a connection, you'll better understand the feedback and can use it moving forward. If not, you might have discovered that members of the team share different views on what the objectives of the product and its design are.

Having a mutually understood foundation or set of objectives is important not just to critique but also to the success of the product and the team. If you discover during a critique that different perspectives about objectives exist within the team, the best course of action is to point it out explicitly. You can then, depending on its severity and the people present, determine if the conversation should change focus to addressing and resolving the difference right then, or if it should be tabled for a separate conversation in the near future.

Participate

One of the best things a designer can do during a critique is to become a critic themselves. Being able to shift our mindset from thinking creatively to being analytical about what we're designing is a key design skill. Participating in a critique of our own work as a critic has multiple benefits.

First, the more we exercise intentionally switching our mindset like this the easier it becomes to control this mindset "toggle." Switching from creative thinking to analytical will be easier, faster, and something we can do whenever we feel like it's helpful, whether we do it by ourselves alone at our desks, or we grab the person sitting next to us for their thoughts, or we schedule a meeting to collect critique from a larger group.

Second, one of the common challenges people have with giving critique is a fear of hurting the designer's feelings. By participating in the analysis and openly talking about the aspects of our design that could be improved upon, we can make others feel more comfortable participating in these discussions.

Third, by modeling the behavior and the form of critique, we demonstrate to the other participants how to give feedback in a way that is helpful to us, making it easier to collect useful critique and facilitate the conversation.

Central Idea

Critique isn't about judgment. It's about analyzing the design so that you can improve it. Participate in that analysis. Listen to the feedback you collect from others and relate it to the objectives of the product you're designing.

Critique, Conversation, and Questions

Good critiques—that is, critiques that are productive for the entire team—are the result of dialogue. The giver and receiver request and exchange information back and forth, and from those exchanges come useful, actionable insights. In a productive critique, there are often a lot of questions asked by both parties.

In fact, great critiques are often more about questions asked than statements made. Questions being asked means that assumptions can be validated, eliminated, or further examined collaboratively. This means that the feedback being collected is based upon a mutually understood foundation rather than each individual's different interpretations. It's also useful for the recipient to pay attention to the questions being asked because they can be signs as to what elements of the design might be unclear or confusing to others.

This should also tell you something about how best to ask for feedback and which communication platforms make the most sense. It's common for designers or teams to send their designs to other members of the team via email and ask for feedback. It's also common for these kinds of exchanges to become problematic.

Email isn't a great conduit for anything resembling real-time conversations. It isn't designed to work that way, but being able to quickly ask questions and get back responses that may assist in advancing your thinking, spur additional questions, or provide insights is crucial. When dealing with multiple people giving feedback, these deficiencies become even more pronounced, because now you need to manage threads, keep track of who gets what information via replies and reply-alls, and so on. We've all likely experienced situations in which feedback was originally solicited by email, and after one or two replies, a conference call or in-person meeting was set up because it just seemed easier than trying to make sense of the lists of questions and comments coming back.

Online feedback tools like inVision and others do their best to try to work around this by making it possible for people to comment on specific aspects of a design and keeping those threads together. This works better, but the non-real-time nature can still prove challenging, because in order to give comments, individuals must do so based on assumptions that they haven't yet been able to validate or eliminate.

That isn't to say that critique isn't possible through these mechanisms. It very much is, but, if we're going to use tools like this, perhaps because we're in a situation for which we have no other choice, we need to ensure that we're doing our best to make them as conversational and focused as possible.

When requesting feedback through a mechanism like this, be specific about what you want feedback on in your request. Specify what the objectives for your product or design were. Allow for as many questions back and forth as you can. When making assumptions in order to offer an insight, be sure to state that assumption so that the recipient can see it and verify that it's true or let you know that it isn't.

It takes more work and can often take a bit longer, but it can be done. We do recommend that, when you can, it's best to use a platform in which everyone can communicate in real time and look at the design together. With some good facilitation (see Chapter 5) you'll find that in sessions like this, whether they're in person or through a conferencing tool like WebEx or Google Hangouts, you'll do much better at collecting useful feedback, keeping the team synchronized, and building a sense of collaboration.

Wrapping Up

Good critique begins with both the giver and recipient having the right intentions: wanting to understand whether the elements of the design will work towards the objectives of the product.

Following are the characteristics that make feedback unhelpful:

- It's driven from personal goals.
- It's untimely.
- It's incomplete.
- It's based on preference.

To help ensure your feedback is useful and works toward improving the product, you should do the following:

- **Lead with questions.** Get more information to base your feedback on and show an interest in their thinking.
- **Use a filter.** Hold on to your initial reactions, investigate them, and discuss them in the proper context, as appropriate.
- **Don't assume.** Determine the thinking or constraints behind choices.
- **Don't invite yourself.** Get in touch and ask to talk about the design.
- **Talk about strengths.** Critique isn't just about what's not working.
- **Think about perspective.** From whose "angle" are you analyzing the design?

Similarly, when asking for feedback, be sure that you aren't do the following:

- Asking with no intention of listening
- Asking when you're really just looking for validation or praise

When asking for critique, keep the following in mind:

- **Remember the purpose.** Critique is about understanding and improvement, not judgment.

- **Listen and think before responding.** Do you understand what the critics are saying and why?

- **Return to the foundation.** Use agreed-upon objectives as a tool to make sure feedback stays focused on objectives.

- **Participate.** Critique the work alongside everyone else.

If we understand the best practices for giving and receiving critique, we also notice a few things about how we collect feedback through various platforms. The more we're able to facilitate real-time question-and-answer sessions across the group, the better the exchange is likely to be. This is why in-person meetings and videoconferencing tend to be best. However, we can still use feedback tools and email; they just take more planning and careful facilitation.

[3]

Culture and Critique

Creating a Conducive Organizational Culture

An organization or team's culture has a huge influence on how critique is incorporated and whether it will be effective. Even if members of a team understand what critique is and have a good grasp of the best practices for giving and receiving it, there are aspects of the culture in which they work that can create obstacles to communication and limit the usefulness and utility of critique.

People, locations, procedures, and more all shape the cultures in which we work. When trying to change any aspect of how people work together within a team, it's important to examine the culture and environment of that team. If you can identify the cultural and environmental aspects that enable or hinder the changes you're trying to make, you have a much better chance at identifying suitable approaches and opportunities for making the changes you're after.

In examining these characteristics with regard to integrating critique, it helps to remember that for the most part when we talk about critique we're talking about a form of communication between two or more people. With that in mind, it makes sense that the characteristics we're most interested in are those that affect who is involved in the communication, what they're communicating about, and when they're communicating.

Organizational politics, territorialism, and influence are significant and common cultural aspects that influence these things, and we'll get to them in a bit. But as Aaron and I have worked with teams to help them strengthen their communication skills, we've observed that two of the most important characteristics of team cultures that indicate whether and where critique will be effective are collaboration and iteration.

COLLABORATION: MORE THAN JUST "WORKING TOGETHER"

Understanding a team's beliefs and approach to collaboration helps us understand with whom critique is most likely to be easy or challenging. Strong facilitation skills can help steer feedback and conversations toward critique—this is an important skill in any organization—but if we want to know who our "critique champions" might be, or the people we might need to throw our best facilitation techniques at, we need to think about how people collaborate and what their attitudes are toward it.

Collaboration itself has a pretty basic definition. Merriam-Webster defines it thus: "to work with another person or group in order to achieve or do something."[1] But those of us who have spent some time collaborating with others on projects know that it isn't quite that simple.

When we examine how people collaborate, we find that there are two primary mechanisms at work, *coordination* and *consensus*. Around each of these we sometimes see extreme versions of collaboration. Teams or individuals that collaborate in these extreme manners tend to present challenges to critique, whereas those that understand the balance between the two do much better.

COORDINATION

Coordination is the act of aligning individual work efforts to produce outcomes that will eventually be assembled into or utilized in the formation of an end product. In these cases, either the individuals are directing their own work or they might be receiving direction from someone else, perhaps a product owner. But that direction and the work done as a result of it is done without much input from or consideration of what others who are working on additional aspects of the solution are doing.

Collaboration at this extreme can be challenging to the integration of critique; if this is how the team members feel they should be collaborating, it's likely they're uncomfortable and/or inexperienced sharing their perspectives on the work of others or having others share perspectives

---

1 Source: *http://www.merriam-webster.com/dictionary/collaborate*

on their own work. These teams or organizations are often separated into silos and have established processes and values that insulate them from one another.

CONSENSUS

On perhaps the other end of the spectrum, we can find collaboration that is contingent entirely on consensus. In these extremes, teams don't do anything unless everyone (or nearly everyone) agrees that it's the right thing to do.

Collaboration of this sort can be challenging for critique, because critique isn't intended to get everyone to agree. Critique is a useful tool for helping to ensure that teams stay focused on what matters most in a project and not getting mired in personal preference. Along those lines, it can help show where there is partial consensus. But its purpose and intention isn't to make everyone agree.

In critiques, people will disagree. Individual perspectives will produce different lines of thinking, and that's OK. If a team feels it needs complete consensus to move forward, a critique won't in any way guarantee that.

MEETING IN THE MIDDLE

The best approaches to collaboration, and by extension those that best support critique, are those that understand that throughout a project, there is a shifting balance between the two mechanisms of coordination and consensus. Leadership—yes, that's still important in collaboration—looks to understand where consensus lies and uses that (but not without still considering any divergent perspectives that might be present) as a basis upon which to make decisions. Also, when appropriate, individuals or groups are able to work in a more coordinated manner to allow for improved efficiency.

In this regard, culturally, members of teams where critique fits easiest are those that exhibit the following:

- A belief that they should offer their perspectives (when appropriate) on what will or will not work for the design the team is creating, even outside of their own skillset or expertise

- A trust that their perspectives will be taken into consideration by whomever is responsible for the aspect of the design being discussed

- The understanding that although their perspective will be taken into consideration, a different direction or decision might be made based on the consideration of other perspectives and relevant expertise and, of course, the objectives of the product

When in a situation that involves their design or an aspect of the design they are responsible for being critiqued, these team members will receive and utilize critique from others such that the preceding three points are supported.

Incremental Versus Iterative Processes: What They Mean and Why They Matter

If a team's collaborative spirit helps us to understand how its culture will influence who is involved in critiques and how we critique with them, its approach to *incremental* and *iterative* processes helps us understand their culture's influence on what they can best critique and when.

Incremental and iterative are adjectives used to describe common design and development processes. As methodologies such as Agile and Lean have become more and more popular, use and discussion of these adjectives has also increased and it's not uncommon for teams to misunderstand or confuse them. Both describe a sequentially based approach to achieving a desired end state for a product, but they employ different means.

INCREMENTAL DESIGN AND DEVELOPMENT

Incremental design and development describes a primarily additive approach to reaching an end state (see Figure 3-1). In an incremental approach, an ultimate solution to the given problem is identified and broken apart into pieces. The time needed to reach the solution's end state—when all of the pieces have been created and assembled together—is divided into phases.

During each phase, a new piece is created and connected to the pieces created in the previous phases. The previously constructed pieces are not modified outside of what is necessary to attach the new piece(s). As a result, the complete creation at the end of any phase is just a collection of all the pieces built so far. Each can still be identified individually because they've changed very little since their original creation.

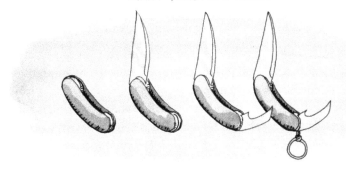

Objective: create a portable, multi-function tool.

FIGURE 3-1
An illustration of incremental design and development if it were applied to a pocket knife

Examples of incremental design, like that depicted in Figure 3-1, feel a bit odd, because teams don't typically release or reveal the product at each intermediate phase. Instead, they wait until the end when all the parts have been assembled.

Another, more well-known example would be to look at organizations working on various products within the same ecosystem. For example, Apple has been working toward a vision of controlling the home/personal media ecosystem. With each new product, iPod, iTunes, Apple TV, countless apps, watches, and so on, the company has moved incrementally closer and closer toward that vision.

In an incremental process, how closely our final creation matches what we had originally intended depends heavily on our ability to think ahead as we build each piece. More important, the effectiveness of our final solution is dependent on how deep our understanding of the problem was when we initially conceived of it.

The rationalization of an incremental approach is that, for most creations, it is too complex and inefficient to try to build the entire solution at once. So, breaking things apart to design and build them in phases makes more sense. The common criticism of incremental approaches is that they require teams to make decisions about what will be created while there are still too many unknowns. Teams must make too many assumptions and base decisions on guesses as to how effective their solutions might be.

ITERATIVE DESIGN AND DEVELOPMENT

Iterative design and development on the other hand recognizes that initial solutions are not likely to be completely effective and therefore the goal is to repeatedly modify a solution to gradually increase its effectiveness.

In this way, iterative approaches can be seen as a recombinatory approach to reaching a final product. With a purely iterative approach, again the timeline is divided into phases, often called *iterations*. A team begins by creating its best attempt at a solution, noting where it is making assumptions. As a solution is created, it is then analyzed to assess its effectiveness, preferably through some interaction with actual users.

Assumptions are either confirmed or disproved. The team now has an updated, more fully formed understanding not just of the effectiveness of its solution but also of the problem(s) that it's trying to solve. It then modifies the solution based on this new knowledge. With each iteration, the solution becomes increasingly more effective.

Examples of iterative processes most resemble evolution. Over time unnecessary or ineffective elements of a product are removed or replaced with new, more fitting or effective elements. For example, consider Figure 3-2, which illustrates the evolution of the telephone from its original design to the cell phone handsets that were around just before smartphones came into being. While these manifestations of the phone are spread out over time and not the result of a single team, they can be seen as iterations on a solution for the objective.

Objective: create a long distance, audio communication device.

FIGURE 3-2

The evolution of the design of the telephone, an example of iteration in design

PROCESSES IN REALITY

In real life, our processes aren't purely incremental or purely iterative. It would be impossible for teams to outright ignore new insights and understandings they gain during a project as they would in a pure incremental approach.

And, a pure iterative approach doesn't allow for teams to break solutions apart into the smaller manageable pieces they need to be able to deliver something.

An effective design and development process is both incremental and iterative. It allows for pieces of a solution to be prioritized and created at different times. Sometimes, those pieces might be identified early in the process but scheduled to be worked on later, as part of a roadmap. Or, sometimes they may come up spontaneously as part of the analysis during iteration.

Additionally, as an iterative approach allows for the solution to be modified with each iteration, new pieces aren't just "bolted on." The overall solution can be changed to incorporate the new pieces in a way that is consistent and makes sense. By combining incremental and iterative approaches, we can work toward a vision while providing repeated opportunities to assess whether our vision is appropriate, learn about the effectiveness of our choices, and modify those choices and our vision, as necessary.

A great example of a combined iterative and incremental process is the creation of this very book. Aaron and I started with a vision, an outline, of what we wanted to create. We then began to write various chapters, building out the book incrementally. At the same time, though, both within each chapter and with the book as a whole, we iterated. We revised sections and chapters and we reorganized things to fit better together, eliminating some sections and discovering a need for some that weren't part of our original vision.

WHY IT MATTERS

So, what do iterative and incremental processes have to do with critique?

Of these two approaches to process, you might guess that iteration is most important to critique, and you'd be right. But just as an effective process will include both iteration and incrementalism, effective critiques will benefit from the same sort of hybrid approach.

For critique to take place, a process must allow for iteration. This is essential, and it's why iteration is such an important aspect of organizational culture. The team's process needs to provide it time to analyze and rethink decisions and change what it designed in the places where it determines the designs won't be effective. Iteration and critique go hand in hand. Critique is a linchpin for iteration. It lets us know how and where to iterate, keeping you on the right track to meeting the objectives of our products.

More than just an allowance by process, the culture of a team must be one that supports and promotes iteration. This means that both individually and as a group, participants need to be comfortable with the idea that what they are analyzing (or what they are presenting to be analyzed) and what will be created as a result of their analysis is only temporary. It provides an opportunity for further analysis and learning, which can then be used to improve the product. Team members need to value continuous improvement over "right-the-first-time," and they need to be working in a process and culture that accommodates and reinforces that value.

If critique is so tied into iteration, why does the incremental process matter? It matters for the same reason that it does in the design and development process: focus. The problems we're trying to solve, or the solutions we're trying to design are often too big to try to discuss, never mind produce, all at once. We need to break them apart and focus on individual pieces at different times. Otherwise, a critique, or any conversation for that matter, can fragment into so many directions that it loses all value.

Central Idea

The cultures that are most conducive to good critique value collaboration and iteration. They understand that for teams to make good decisions together, critical thinking is necessary, and that to accommodate critique and continuous improvement, iteration must be supported.

ORGANIZATIONAL POLITICS, TERRITORIALISM, AND INFLUENCE

Examining both of the previously noted cultural aspects further, in particular the attitudes and behaviors of individuals related to them, can begin to touch upon the uglier sides of organizational culture that many of us know and often loathe. Politics, territorialism, and influence based upon position and organizational hierarchy can have a huge impact on critique and communication as a whole.

Politics and social taboos influence how we communicate with one another and can create barriers to critique. Team members can withhold valuable insights due to intimidation by other team members and leaders, or for fear of being labeled negatively. If team members repeatedly have been told "no" in the past, they might not feel as though their insights are valued and therefore not contribute. It is our job to work past these cultural barriers and help team members and clients contribute in a positive way.

> I once worked at a company where product design teams were competing with one another, vying for resources and funding for their projects. This created a very political culture in which teams were not focusing on what was best for the company and products but were instead concentrating on getting recognition for themselves, even at the expense of others. Secrecy and combativeness were common in meetings and critiques.
>
> I sat in critiques during which managers gave harsh criticisms on work that another manager's team had done because it was getting more attention than their projects, or because that manager had said something negative that affected them in the past. This not only created an environment in which collaboration was sparse and communication was fragmented, but it discouraged team members from participating in critiques.
>
> **—AARON**

Bringing about change in politically charged and territorial cultures like this can be difficult, but it can be done. Observation is our ally. Notice who the positive contributors are and establish relationships with them. Positive contributors are those team members who have the product's (and its users') best interest at heart and will be advocates for better processes that lead to positive results for the product. We can work with them using the tools we have to establish a solid foundation for critique and communication (see the section "Setting the Foundation for Critique" coming up shortly) to build toward more objective-focused conversations. When the focus is on the product and its objectives, and not on individual agendas, it becomes easier to cultivate a healthy environment for critique.

This is not a walk in the park. You need to work toward an established (and realistic) goal and be prepared to accept incremental change.

Setting the Foundation for Critique

To help ensure that we are integrating critique to the best of our ability, we need to work at building a culture in which the conversations surrounding design are productive. When working to change culture, whether it's to make it more conducive to critique or to achieve any kind of shift, it's important to know that there aren't big, quick solutions.

Culture is pervasive. Not only is it the shared values and behaviors of a group, it's also directly reinforced by the group's actions and behaviors. This chicken-or-egg scenario makes culture change difficult to do in large waves. Instead, it's important to identify and implement small changes that have lasting effect.

One such change is in the establishment of a shared foundation for any project. In the organizations Aaron and I have found that are most effective in their communication and critique, we've seen that all of them begin their projects by explicitly identifying the objectives of the project to a significant degree of detail. It seems completely logical, but you'd be surprised at how many teams we've encountered that when we've asked them what the objectives are of the product their designing, very few people are able to answer, and those who do rarely answer with the same objectives.

LACK OF FOUNDATION

Conversations that happen during the design process can often go awry because the participants all have varying ideas, visions, and goals in mind. The framing of dialogues and discussions for each team member is then different because they're working toward a different set of objectives from the others.

Have you ever attended a meeting in which it seems like everyone has their own agenda or concept of the direction in which the product should be going, but none of them really line up? Or perhaps in the meeting it seemed like everyone was talking about the same thing and left with their to-do's, but when you reconvened, it was clear by the work everyone had done that they had a very different idea of what had been discussed?

This environment has a huge influence on critique because all of the members are working toward their own individual ideas of where the product should go or how it should be built. If teams in these situations do try to critique, it's often ineffective because the objectives each participant is critiquing against are different.

> I recall attending a meeting during which we were reviewing some design work, and the feedback from almost every individual on the team was different. One product owner thought a feature should be changed to make an internal team work more efficiently, an executive wanted to make changes to the feature so that there would be less development work, and a designer wanted to take what they were building in a direction that they thought was innovative. Each individual had valid points, but each point was being pursued separate of the other. There was no foundation set that tied all of these insights together, nothing to turn to as a North Star to prioritize things and guide the conversation and ensure that we stayed on the right path.
>
> **—AARON**

Different perspectives among team members aren't a bad thing. It's why we work in teams—to harness a wider array of insights and expertise. But, there needs to be some level setting, a foundation that comprises common goals and a shared understanding. When everyone is on the same page, the unique experience, vision, and goals of each team member can work in harmony for the good of the process and ultimately the product.

CREATING AN EFFECTIVE, COMMON FOUNDATION

What goes into a solid foundation? What kinds of things should teams work toward agreeing on before diving into the design?

There are four common and widely used tools: personas, scenarios, goals and principles, that when put together, create a solid foundation. These tools help us guide our conversations a provide points of reference to keep everyone on the same page throughout the process.

When Aaron and I talk about the objectives of a project or product, it is typically these 4 things that we are referring to. The objectives for a product are to:

- Reach its goals...

- For the given audiences (personas)...

- By creating a design with the right behaviors and characteristics (principles)...

- To produce the desired experience when used in the applicable contexts (scenarios).

The background: personas and scenarios

Personas and scenarios provide the "setting" for the analysis? How are we going to look at the design? Through whose eyes? With what behaviors or expectations? In what contexts?

Personas are user archetypes that describe an individual's behaviors, goals, expectations, knowledge, and so on (see Figure 3-3). There are lots of opinions on the depth and details to include in personas; our preference is to use half-page, succinct personas that list main points (with elaborations as appropriate) that can be referenced at a glance as opposed to deeper, narrative-style personas.

A word of caution regarding personas: stay focused on what matters and be explicit. Many teams get carried away including details that don't matter, aren't helpful, or aren't explicit enough. For example, is it really important to include that your persona has two dogs and enjoys spending his Saturdays in the park? What does that tell the team? Don't use flowery stories or superfluous details to hint at characteristics or behaviors, state them explicitly.

Similarly, don't get hung up on demographics. Demographics are often used as stereotypes for behaviors and characteristics. For example, persona Steph is a millennial; therefore, she must be great with technology. That's not necessarily true. Aaron and I know quite a few millennials who are absolutely clueless about technology. Just as we know many people over the age of 60, a demographic often assumed to be technology-challenged, who are far better than Adam with computers, and his degree is in computer science.

The Occasional Consumer

Fredrick Loren
Age: 31
Role: Web Designer/Developer
Years in Role: 4

CONSUMPTION BEHAVIORS

* Uses Google Reader and has subscriptions to 100+ blogs.
* Rarely reads actual posts, 3-5 per week tops
* Searches for content most often when he has an immediate use for it
* Uses Reader as another content repository when looking for content on a topic
* Searches split 50/50 between performed on laptop vs on iPhone
* Consumption done most often on laptop

SHARING BEHAVIORS

* Has Twitter and Facebook accounts.
* Posts infrequently
* Shares even more infrequently and only does so with vague comments like "This is awesome."

LEARNING/READING BEHAVIORS

* Learns by doing.
* Gets frustrated with long explanations, and therefore often skips over them.
* Doesn't often set aside time for learning, Looks things up "in the moment"
* Often takes example code and files and manipulates to meet his needs in order to understand how things are working

IN FRED'S WORDS...

I'm a web designer at Stratford Mutual Financial Group tasked with helping design tools for our agents to help them sell annuities, life insurance and retirement planning to consumers.

The agents are a demanding audience who are constantly frustrated with how slow Stratford Mutual is in keeping up with technology. They often go out and buy the newest gadgets (phones, tablets, etc.) and immediately question why we don't have apps/tools/support for it.

As such, my past few projects have all had something to do with new technologies, in particular mobile and responsive design and development.

FIGURE 3-3

An example of a persona used in a project for the creation of a new knowledge-sharing platform

The point is, learn the real characteristics of your audience and state them explicitly in your personas to help minimize any confusion or misunderstandings as they're referenced throughout the project.

Scenarios are short narratives that describe the contexts in which your product will be used and the experience people have when using it (see Figure 3-4). Scenarios aren't limited to include only what the user does, or what the product does. They aim to capture the full experience including an individual's thought process and emotions.

Similar to personas, it's not uncommon for teams to become caught up in the fun of storytelling when writing scenarios. Base your scenarios on real observations. Be sure that the details you include matter. When you include a thought, emotion, or reaction that the user might have while using your product, make sure it's something meaningful that you intend for your design to either address or produce.

In the design community it's common to hear or use phrases like "I/ You are not the user." But, this can be hard for people to remember; clients and professionals with other areas of expertise—hey, sometimes even designers themselves—forget it for a moment or two.

By setting up solid personas and scenarios at the beginning of your project (hopefully based on research) you give yourself and your team a starting point to help guide your critique and analysis.

FRED LOOKS FOR SOMETHING ON RESPONSIVE WEB DESIGN

Fred is designing and prototyping a responsive web app for Stratford Mutual's agents. Fred feels like the navigation for the app is too much to display at once, so as he codes a prototype, he wants to try out a collapsible menu that would slide down from the top of the screen when dragged. He's seen it on a number of other sites, so he knows it can be done, but has never done it himself. **He needs to find a resource to help him do it.**

Luckily, Stratford Mutual uses MindMerge, a media-library and knowledge-sharing tool that allows him to search for information on topics others in his company have used and found useful.

There's a meeting in about 37 minutes and Fred wants to have this new nav in place to show there so he can get his team's feedback. So he opens up MindMerge and looks for something to help him get his menu working.

After a quick search on "responsive web navigation," the system presents Fred with a set of prioritized results. From the results screen Fred can see that there are extra details that help him understand if the item might be useful to him.

Fred selects one that looks like it has code samples. He opens it and scans it quickly to see if it does what he needs. It looks like it does, so he copies the code into his prototype. Tests it and heads off to his meeting.

How does MindMerge allow Fred to search for the information he's after and choose the items that best fit his needs right now?

CONSIDER THE FOLLOWING

- Fred doesn't have a lot of time and is looking to put this information to use right now.
- How does the system present prioritized results based on Fred's needs and preferences?
- What kind of information does MindMerge include in it's search results to help Fred know if a particular result might meet his needs and be useful to him?
- What kinds of options or information does the system give Fred if he can't find something that's useful in the search results?
- How does the system make use of the fact that Fred used the content and learned what he needed to so that it can better position that content for other MindMerge users?

FIGURE 3-4

Part of a scenario used in a project for the creation of a new knowledge-sharing platform

Personas Help Visual Design Discussions, Too

Most people are familiar with the idea of using personas and scenarios for interaction design, but they don't realize how effective these tools can be in discussing visual design. Several years ago, I was coaching a team of two interaction designers and a visual designer working on an enterprise software

Kim Goodwin,
Consultant,
VP of UX at
PatientsLikeMe

product. As the visual designer began transforming sketches into pixels, the interaction designers would look over his shoulder and ask him to change specific things about the color, type, or layout. When he disagreed, they tried to use a persona as a sort of trump card: "Trust us, we did the user research." The designer felt disrespected because his peers weren't listening and, even worse, were trying to art direct his work. At the same time, the two interaction designers were frustrated because they felt he was making design choices based on his own preferences and then getting defensive about them. Trust and respect were quickly eroding.

As it turns out, designers can get just as stuck on their personal opinions as anyone else. This is especially true if they don't use the same evaluation criteria for a design solution. Teams sometimes think evaluation criteria are "shared" as long as they're written down somewhere or mentioned in a meeting. It's not that easy. Evaluation criteria are not truly shared unless everyone both understands them and believes in them. In this anecdote, the visual designer had limited involvement in both the user research and the scenario development. This is sometimes necessary from a budget standpoint, but his teammates could have done more to get him involved.

Shared criteria are especially difficult to develop for the emotionally expressive aspects of a solution, such as the visual or physical styling of a product, because it simply feels so much more subjective than something like workflow. People also struggle when they don't have the language for describing problems with the design. This is why the interaction designers fell back on trying to dictate solutions: they just didn't know how else to express themselves. On the other side, frustrated feedback recipients are less inclined to tease out exactly what the real (and often valid) concern is.

The visual designer was juggling two projects and couldn't spend much more time with the interaction designers, but a few simple communication approaches helped the team get along while making the most of everyone's expertise.

Use emotional goals to drive visual style and voice

Like real humans, effective personas have not only practical goals about what they want to accomplish, but also goals about how they want to feel (in general and at particular points in their journeys). Using these to both guide and evaluate the visual style turned the team's discussion from personal preference to whether orange-and-lime-green or a casual typeface would really inspire enough confidence in the product. And by the way, this works for the tone of your copy, too.

Use scenarios to articulate visual hierarchy needs

The interaction designers were mostly concerned about visual hierarchy—what was emphasized and de-emphasized on the screen—but they didn't have the right language to express themselves. The next time they reviewed a set of scenario storyboards with the visual designer, I asked them to discuss several things. Who's the most important persona for this scenario? What's the first thing that persona should see or notice on the screen? What should the persona notice after that? Which things on the screen should the persona notice only by exception, or when more detail becomes necessary? This helped the visual designer get the visual hierarchy right the first time.

Keep asking: which persona, which scenario, which goal?

After the first two approaches restored enough good will, the team members were ready to listen to one another again. When someone offered a solution instead of a concern, his colleagues would ask questions like, which persona or scenario are you thinking about? When you say this style isn't working, what seems contrary to which emotional goal? This let the team agree on the problem, so everyone felt heard and respected.

It's tempting to use personas and goals like hammers to end arguments, but this can backfire if the other person isn't fully invested in the personas, or you haven't fully understood their concern. Personas are much more effective when used as tools to clarify understanding and as conversational shorthand for complex needs and behaviors.

The end game: goals and principles

If personas and scenarios are the starting point, goals and principles are the finish line. Goals and principles describe where you're trying to go with the design; they outline the future you're trying to create and ways in which you want to create it. For whatever aspect of a design you're critiquing, you can ask of them, "Does this help us reach our goal of..." or "Does this adhere to the principle of _____ that we set?" followed by "How?" and "Why?"

Goals are the desired, measurable outcomes that result from the product being used. Figure 3-5 demonstrates how they help capture the difference between the current world and the future world.

DESIGN GOALS

- **Decrease time spent researching** topics by 15%.
- **Increase utilization** of purchased education & reference materials by 20%.
- **Identify** materials not being used so that they may be eliminated for cost-savings.

FIGURE 3-5
Example goals for a new knowledge-sharing platform

The team should feel that the goals set forth are achievable and meaningful and that they should correlate to a change in user behavior. It's also best to avoid goals that are binary or output based. For example, a goal of adding a "remember me" feature to a login screen is about output. It's binary in that the team either produces it or it doesn't. A better goal would be "increase authenticated visits to our site by 15 percent."

Principles are the qualities and characteristics that the product will exhibit in its content, behavior, and so on as people use it and interact with it, as shown in Figure 3-6.

DESIGN PRINCIPLES

- **Be where I am**. Don't be just another place I have to go log into. The further out of my way I have to go to use the tool, the less likely I am to use it.
- **Know me.** What are my interests? Go beyond "topics." Understand my preferences in other facets (length, content type, style, etc.)
- **Not everyone is equal.** Understand that some people's recommendations mean more than others.

FIGURE 3-6
Example principles for a new knowledge-sharing platform

Good principles should be somewhat specific. Characteristics like "fun" or "amusing" don't make great design principles because they're still pretty broad. Every member of a team might have a different interpretation of what "fun" is.

Good principles also act as constraints and filtering mechanisms for detailed design ideas. By virtue of being specific, a good design principle helps you to eliminate more design ideas than you retain from idea-generation activities such as brainstorms, which allows you to focus your efforts as you move forward.

Similar to personas and scenarios, if your team knows the goals and principles, if it understands and agrees to them, goals and principles act as a tool to keep your critiques on track. With them, you can keep the discussion focused on learning things that will help you iteratively improve your design and move closer to achieving the desired end state.

It's important to ensure that your team understands all of the foundational elements you're addressing. This way, when comments come up in a critique that feel like they're based on a personal preference, or something outside the foundation you're designing for, you can refer back to the applicable personas/scenarios/goals/principles and scenarios and ask how the comment relates to them.

If it does, great! That means that people are still critiquing from the foundation you set.

If not, you can move the critique along to the next comment. Or, perhaps you need to discuss whether the comment really matters and should be factored into the design. It is possible to miss something when establishing a foundation. Moreover, new information can come up during the course of a project that can change the importance of foundational elements or even reveal new ones. But by starting your project with them, you have a basis for discussing whether these comments indicate that something might be missing.

MAKING IT LAST: THE MINI CREATIVE BRIEF

The foundation starts your project off on the right foot, but its real effectiveness in changing process and culture lies in carrying it through into discussions throughout the project. It's a colossal waste when teams spend tons of time at the beginning of a project crafting goals, scenarios, and so on and then two months later, when they're in the heat of design, no one can remember the last time anyone actually looked at or talked about a persona or other key foundational objective.

A great tool for keeping the foundation in front of the team throughout the project is a *Mini Creative Brief.* Maybe you haven't experienced this, but almost every creative brief we have come across is the opposite of "brief." As such, it's pretty quickly discarded, because referring to it is painful.

We first learned of this technique from Jared Spool, the founder of User Interface Engineering (UIE), who in turn was introduced to it by one of his clients. The idea behind the Mini Creative Brief is to capture the most important foundational elements and objectives for the product on a single page or less. Using the foundational elements above, a Mini Creative Brief would include the following:

- A brief summary of the problem statement or purpose of the product

- The key users (personas) of the solution

- The main scenarios in which the solution will be used

- The business goals that have been established for the product

- The design principles to be followed

Keep in mind that this is a mini brief, so it is not necessary that we have the full documentation of these items; instead, they should be high-level lists and summaries that convey keep points to the team.

As you are starting meetings or having discussions about designs, take a few minutes to review the Mini Creative Brief with the team. This acts as a reminder and focusing mechanism so that conversations are centered and everyone is on the same page. The team at UIE even goes so far as to have someone different read the Mini Creative Brief aloud at the beginning of each meeting to ensure that the information is being read by people from across the team, not just a project lead or designer. You can read more about the Mini Creative Brief on the UIE blog at *http://www.uie.com/articles/short_form_creative_brief/.*

Central Idea

Keeping critiques focused on what matters for the product means having a mutually understood set of objectives. By working to uncover what these are and referencing them regularly throughout a project we not only have better critiques, but we begin to change the culture and dynamics of a team to better support critique.

PUTTING THESE TOOLS TO USE

All of these tools are your allies. Center your conversations on them and use them to build a foundation for stronger critiques. As you create and gather these tools, be sure that you not only share them with your team, but also keep them posted and accessible in shared repositories such as Dropbox or a wiki. Consider putting them up on walls in a shared workspace if you can; this will help increase their visibility to the team. There's truth to the cliché, "Out of sight, out of mind." So, make an effort to keep these things in sight and, more important, in conversation.

Personal Barriers to Critique

Even with a supportive culture and a good foundation in place, there are other obstacles that can hinder our ability to integrate critique. Individuals on their own have a number of factors that affect how they communicate with one another and whether they might have difficulty with critique or not.

ADDITIONAL CULTURAL INFLUENCES

Outside of organizational culture, the societal and ethnic cultures that an individual is a part of affect how they communicate in team settings. For example, many of us are raised to abide by the principle, "If you don't have anything nice to say, don't say anything at all." There are many people who, not wanting to hurt someone's feelings during a critique session, hold back from delivering honest critique that they worry might upset the recipient. Or worse, they validate ideas even if they think it isn't the right direction. Being honest can be difficult, but it's also essential to good critique.

In some cultures challenging or speaking up is seen as rude, whereas other cultures are more open, straightforward, and abrupt. These kinds of differences can lead to misunderstandings. People might sense that others who are more used to being straightforward are actually being combative. Or participants might think that people who tend to refrain from sharing disagreement in groups are in agreement.

Respect and trust are tantamount to good critique. We need to consider these influences when preparing for critiques and, if necessary, communicate to those who will be participating that it is perfectly acceptable for them to step outside of these "norms." We should ensure that everyone knows that when sharing thoughts and insights during the critique, it is not a reflection on the designer(s) skills or expertise; rather, it is part of the process of analyzing whether what we are working on is on track to reach the goals we set for it. It is safe to say that if someone shares thoughts that your design is not working in some way or another, you are probably still a good person. Critique is about understanding and improvement, not judgment.

It's not only our societal mores that affect what we share; the language differences that are part of our cultures can cause obstacles, too.

> I'll never forget the first time I worked with a team from India. About a month into the project, the team came to our offices to work with us onsite. All of the team members were wonderful people, but after our meetings, I kept finding out that we weren't as aligned as I had thought we were during the meetings, or that where I thought there had been disagreement there actually wasn't any. It turned out that I misread some of their body language; what I thought meant one thing, actually meant something different to them.
>
> **—ADAM**

Different cultures and regions sometimes use words or gestures to mean different things. These kinds of gaps in communication can become apparent in team communication and critique, so it's important to try to identify and clarify them as soon as they're noticed.

NEGATIVE CRITIQUE EXPERIENCES

In the same way that an individual's societal, ethnic, and cultural influences can affect how he communicates with teams and clients in a critique setting, any past experiences with critique can also affect how one participates in sessions.

Putting your work out there for other people to analyze or comment on is intimidating enough in and of itself, but if you have had negative experiences with it in the past that sense of intimidation is heightened. We have all heard horror stories from designers who were taught to have "thick skin" by professors in college who used "critique" as an opportunity to break them down, which reminds me of a story that a designer told me recently while we were discussing critique.

> I was in RISD Graphic Design. On our first project we had to design a form. Not a lot of setup, we had a few hours. I thought I'd make my form slanted up to the right—like how people actually write. We are all instructed to tape them on the wall. The teacher (a well-known designer) walks straight up to mine, tears it off the wall, throws it on the floor, and stomps on it, all the while saying absolutely nothing.
>
> I was too embarrassed to say anything.
>
> **—DORELLE RABINOWITZ**

Although we understand the need for having thick skin as a designer, this is surely not the way to teach it.

Critique should be a safe, collaborative environment, in which teams can discuss their designs among themselves, with clients, and with others within their organizations. We can help create this environment by setting certain rules for critiques (these are discussed at greater length in Chapter 5) and ensuring that everyone is aware of them.

FOSTERING THE ABILITY TO COMMUNICATE

Not everyone communicates in the same way—there are actually people who are not good at communicating at all. Communication is a vital component to critique and when communication is off, the chances of having productive critiques are minimal at best.

It would be silly to think that we must improve everyone's ability to communicate before starting our critiques; if that were the case, we might never start. Teammates' communication skills will improve as they grow better at critiquing, and we can help them. To begin, observe them, clients, and business partners to see how they communicate, and then see what they respond to positively and negatively. We can then use these insights to help structure our communication with them as well as use them to improve the way we facilitate our critiques.

As we continue to learn and understand how various team members communicate we can begin to plan how we want to use our tools for facilitating critique with team members who communicate in different ways. We may need to approach those who might be difficult or tend to dominate discussions in a one-on-one setting and share our ideas for how critique should work. Setting expectations up front is helpful in avoiding conflict during the critique session.

Adam and I have also found it helpful to approach those within the team who communicate well and share the vision for how we would like to see critique work. As they understand the value, they can help in communicating that value to the rest of the team as well as be a support during the critique session. Going it alone is not easy, so find advocates and allies.

We shared some helpful tools earlier in this chapter. Don't hesitate to distribute these to your teammates before the critiques happen so that they can review them and ask any questions. The conversation about what we are critiquing should begin before the actual meeting. Share the rules and process that you want to establish for your critique sessions (see Chapter 4 for a more in-depth explanation of the rules for critique) so teammates can know what to expect going in.

By providing your teammates with a framework for how to you want to communicate insights and ask questions during the critique, you provide them the opportunity to work past communication issues and contribute effectively.

Central Idea

An individual's own history, culture, and capabilities influence her ability to critique effectively with others and her attitudes toward it. If you truly value critique and collaboration, you should take measures to work with individuals, identify and address communication gaps, and ensure that they feel safe in sharing their work and perspectives.

Practicing Critique

As we've described, changing aspects of culture is not a once-and-done endeavor. Any effective approach requires longevity and reinforcement. And as with any skill, the act of practice, whether intentional or not, is critical to improvement.

By finding as many opportunities to critique, no matter how formal or informal, you not only improve people's critiquing skills, you also build an awareness of critique and make it a more natural component of your team's conversations—effectively changing the culture.

We suggest that you start small, working with one or two others to get used to having dialogues about your designs. Do this as often as you can so that you can get comfortable in a critique setting and work up to larger groups from there.

One tactic to help get your team comfortable and adjusted to how critique differs from other feedback is to critique competitor's designs; this is not only helpful with respect to competitive analysis, but it also provides a forum in which the team can practice the critique process.

I had a design director with whom I worked closely, and at the end of every day, we would set aside some time to talk about the work we did that day and to offer each other critique. This helped us become comfortable discussing our work with each other and, more important, become comfortable with someone critiquing our work. Every so often we would include our product manager and even developers, helping us to get used to multiple points of view.

In the end, it really does come down to practice, practice, practice, and then after that, practice some more. Some things will work, others won't; the more you practice critiquing with your team, the more you will begin to understand what will work best. Much of what we are sharing in the book we learned through trial and error, eventually getting to what worked best.

Central Idea

Critique is a skill. It must be practiced. Don't expect it to be perfect the first time you try it. Find as many opportunities as you can to do it, and over time, things will get better as you go.

Critiquing with Distributed Teams and Remote Team Members

Telecommuting and geographically separated teams are a reality and becoming more and more common. Sadly, many people still view them as a kiss-of-death to any hope of good collaboration or communication. But collaboration is a mindset, not a by-product of co-location. So long as that mindset is present, with a few tricks and the right tools, remote team members can contribute to a critique just as well as the teammate sitting in the room with us.

Both Aaron and I work remotely. The product design team that Aaron works with has a mixture of co-located and distributed team members spread out across different company and home offices. They have a very collaborative structure and design process with design studio and critique at the center. Nothing is ever as fun as being in the same room with someone, but when that is not an option, the quality of collaborative activities and critiques does not need to suffer. They have equally effective critique sessions with team members both in-office and remotely. It really comes down to having a shared understanding of critique's importance in the process and the mindset to make it work.

The first challenge to overcome in remote arrangements is the lack of nonverbal communication that we get with the ever-popular phone or conference call. Hearing someone's voice lets us know what someone is saying, but we miss so much of the information that comes from seeing the person say it. The solution to this is pretty easy: video chat. This technology goes a long way toward giving us the nonverbal information we need as we collaborate. With it, we can see facial expressions, gestures, posture, all the things we would pick up if you were in the same room with the individual.

Screen sharing makes it possible for us to focus a group's attention on a single artifact or visual, something very important to collaborative activities. In a critique, we can share documents in a format such as PDF and then, using Adobe Acrobat, add comments directly on the pages using the commenting feature. Or we can use a program such as InVision with which we can share and comment as we talk through designs with our teams.

For instances in which we need more freeform visualizing and capturing of ideas, like the kind of freedom we get from a nice clean whiteboard, a fresh pack of dry erase markers, and a pile of sticky note pads, try using tools such as BoardThing, StormBoard, and document cameras (we like iPevo's) in conjunction with screen sharing. Document cameras are webcams that are built for sharing documents and live transcription or note-taking, similar to the overhead projectors some of us are familiar with from elementary school. With them, we can sketch and annotate in real time with teammates, or share sketches that we have previously worked on.

There are many other tools available for remote collaboration, and more being released almost daily. Because of the reality that many coworkers aren't actually co-located, and the growing interest in telecommuting, many companies are looking to make collaborating from separate locations as much like being in the same room as possible.

More important than the tools we use, however, is our approach. For remote collaboration to work, the individuals involved have to want to make it work. They have to believe in the importance of collaboration, be conscious of the differences being remote poses, and address them together. So long as our team is dedicated to making critique and collaboration work in remote settings, we will find a way.

Hallway Conversations Without the Hallways

When I switched to full-time remote work, I knew the lack of chats in the kitchen and nods in the hall would leave me longing for human connection. So, I added a book club and some dinner gatherings to my life outside of work, and I expected things to be more or less under control.

Veronica Erb,
Designer at NPR

What I didn't realize, however, was how important those inadvertent interactions with coworkers were to feeling comfortable both giving and receiving critique.

Suddenly, nearly all of my time with coworkers was spent in design reviews or status meetings. By its very nature, critique reminds us of the things we haven't yet done. And so, though the "no's" and "not yets" were helping me create better designs, they were also more prominent in my mind than the occasional reminders that I was a valued and welcome part of the team.

It had a terrible effect on my psyche. My inner critic ran rampant. "This can't be the most efficient way of doing it." "You're not as productive as so-and-so." At its worst, it declared, "They'll figure out you swindled them into hiring you!" Because I had little idea of what my coworkers' pace or methods were, I believed her. I couldn't see any evidence contrary to my inner critic's accusations.

My crumbling self-confidence meant that I was less and less likely to offer my insights to peers and that their critique felt more and more about my worth instead of about my designs.

Later, after I started a project where I was regularly collaborating with a small team, I found out that similar thoughts occurred to them during their remote work life. Rather than sliding into the bathrobe-wearing slovenly person so many conjure when they imagine remote work, we were each turning into paranoid workaholics. The culprit was our insufficient trust building outside of critique.

The discovery from our commiseration gave me the courage to consciously pursue connection with my team. Here are some tactics that have helped me:

Waste some meeting time

Spend a few minutes at the beginning or the end of a meeting having hallway conversations without the hallway. Pairing conversation with critique reminds us that we're all on the same team.

Broadcast a little

Allow coworkers to "notice" your homemade curry lunch or your new paper prototyping kit through whatever shared communication your team has, such as Twitter, Slack, or IRC. Discovering similarities with coworkers builds connection.

Bond individually

Swap stories and catch up during video chat lunches. They're even easier to schedule than in-person lunches, and one on one time strengthens bonds.

Perfect your remote walk-by

Asking for spontaneous critique is the most difficult to adapt to remote work. A quick "Got a minute?" instant message is a good place to start. Be sure to jump on a voice or video call when you need it.

Practicing a mix of these tactics and others enabled me to improve the trust we felt as a team. That trust builds the foundation required for productive critique.

Whatever you do, give yourself permission to experiment. Getting it right in the remote world will take some work, and you and your team are worth it.

Central Idea

While remote and telecommuting arrangements pose challenges to collaboration and critique, remember that collaboration is a mindset, not a result of co-location. If team members value collaboration, with tools like video chat and screen sharing, remote collaboration and critique sessions can be just as effective as they are in person.

Wrapping Up

Collaboration and iteration are key elements in organizational cultures where critique is successful. Cultures that best support critique are those that value collaboration and iteration.

Other aspects of organizational culture, such as politics and territorialism, also influence a team's ability to critique. To counter these aspects and work to change the culture we can set a foundation for our projects that consists of personas, scenarios, goals, and principles.

Collecting these foundational elements and referring to them regularly through a tool such as a Mini Creative Brief helps to keep conversations focused on what's important.

Additional obstacles to critique can arise from each individual's own experiences and culture. To address these, do the following:

- Set expectations up front. Let people know that they are expected to be honest and share their perspectives.

- If you need to, reaching out to those who you know will be participating to gauge their previous critique experiences will help in identifying any members with whom you might need to have additional conversations in preparation for critiques.

- Be on the lookout for differences in understanding. Sometimes, it isn't immediately obvious that they're happening. Often, people think they're talking about the same thing only to find out later they had completely different interpretations.

Working remotely offers some additional challenges to collaboration and, by extension, critique. But there are many tools available today, and more being released all the time that help overcome these challenges. Video chat, screen sharing, digital whiteboards, and document cameras go a long way to providing the capabilities we need to critique effectively when we can't be in the same space.

Change doesn't happen overnight. It will take some time to get it right, so set reasonable goals for yourself and your team and practice, practice, practice. Repetition and reinforcement are crucial to changing culture.

[4]

Making Critique a Part of Your Process

Creating Opportunities for Critique

Critique is an analysis tool that we use for the purposes of evolving and improving something. At any point during our projects—when we're looking to take what we have created so far and analyze it in order to make it better by revising choices we might have made—we have an opportunity for critique.

As Aaron and I have worked with organizations to see how they are or aren't using critique, we've found three common points in processes during which feedback is often collected. These points offer some interesting opportunities and considerations for critique.

Standalone critiques
> Meetings or discussions held for the sole purposed of critiquing something

Collaborative activities
> Events in which multiple people work together simultaneously to solve a specific challenge

Design reviews
> A common event in organizations' project and design processes

Things to Keep in Mind

We'll discuss each of the above forms in more depth later in this chapter, but before we do, it's important to call out some considerations that you should keep in mind as any team works to incorporate critique into their process or improve upon the way you might already be using critique.

START SMALL

The number of people involved has a direct effect on how much effort it takes to manage a conversation, both from a facilitation standpoint as well as an individual participant's ability to follow along.

When introducing critique or working on improving an organization's skills with it, it's good to keep the number of people involved to fewer at first, maybe just pairs. This minimizes the mental acrobatics that participants need to do to keep track of everyone's feedback and gives them the ability to focus a bit more on the critique itself and their own skills within it. As people grow more comfortable, you can introduce increasingly larger groups.

THINK BEFORE YOU SPEAK

Listening plays a huge role in critique, for both recipients and those giving the feedback. It's been beaten into many of us that there is a difference between listening and hearing. That difference can become very clear in conversations, particularly discussions that include or are focused on feedback.

Hearing is a passive act. It's something that we just do. And even though it takes no real effort for us "hear" something, it can still produce a response. At any given moment, we're likely to be hearing a variety of things, some influencing our actions and some not, all with little to no conscious recognition of what we're hearing actually is or means. We still react to what we hear, but these reactions are typically impulsive and automatic. Does that sound like anything we've already discussed?

Listening, on the other hand, requires focus. When we listen, we take in information through what we're hearing and consciously interpret it to form an understanding that directs how we behave. This process is a deliberate one that we're aware of as it is happening. We're conscious of the questions being asked in our brain to make sense of what we've heard and we're focusing our energy on getting to that interpretation.

Although both hearing and listening can lead to changes in action and both rely on some form of attention, it's this deliberate focus and conscious awareness that separates listening from hearing. To make sure our feedback discussions stay focused on pertinent, useful feedback, we need to ensure that we've actually listened to and understood what has been said before we say something in response. Whether you are giving or receiving critique, listening plays a critical role.

THINK ABOUT WHO TO INCLUDE

When working on an organization's critique skills, it's important to give some consideration to which individuals you bring into the conversations, given that each participant can either help or hinder the others. This in no way means that we should start excluding everyone who might be struggling. It's more that we need to think about how and why we put people together in critiques whose purpose is to maximize the potential for improving the skills of the group overall.

OK. With all that now out of the way, let's talk about process. Or, more specifically, the ways critique can fit into it.

Central Idea

Regardless of how and when you incorporate critique, be intentional. Think about who should be included. Keep groups small when first introducing critique. And always, listen and think before you speak.

Standalone Critiques

Standalone critiques are nothing more than meetings or discussions with the single purpose of critiquing a creation so that it can be iterated upon further. This form makes it possible for us to critique pretty much anything we need analysis on, at any time. Because of that flexibility they often provide us with the ability to gather more targeted and focused feedback on specific areas of our designs than we would if we wait and try to incorporate feedback into other project meetings.

> At a previous job, my director and I would chat at the end of every day to discuss the work we did, how we felt about it, and provide each other with feedback. On one particular project, we had a tight deadline and a lot of ambiguity surrounding the website we needed to design. Because we met at the end of each day for critique, we were able to talk through our design decisions and help each other measure those decisions against our goals. The more we met, the better we became at asking questions about each other's work as well as uncovering

questions to ask the product team so we could get the information we felt was lost in ambiguity. After the project, we continued meeting at the end of each day, and once or twice a week, we included a product manager to help build a shared understanding.

This was very helpful to both of us because we became very comfortable giving and receiving feedback and it also helped us improve our presentation and communication skills when discussing designs. It also didn't hurt that a nice cold beer often accompanied these standalone critiques.

—AARON

Standalone critiques are also very effective when we're introducing critique to someone who isn't familiar with the process or when a team is working to practice and improve its critique skills. Because the entire purpose of these meetings is to critique something, we can organize them so that they provide a safe, controlled place in which participants can share and analyze work while getting comfortable with giving and receiving feedback. This is especially helpful when we're working with teammates who might be intimidated by receiving or giving feedback, possibly because they have had negative experiences with it in the past. It truly is awesome to watch someone come out of his shell as he improves his ability to communicate ideas and designs to others, receive feedback on his work, and use that feedback to strengthen his creations.

Continuous Critique

Russ Unger, Director, Experience Design Center of Excellence at 18F

"Team critique" likely sets a nice visual—a lot of people gathered in a semicircle around a wall adorned with beautiful designs. Inevitably, someone is pointing at a particular design, while others hover back a bit with furrowed brows and questions on the tips of their tongues. It looks like a fun scenario to get to be a part of!

The reality that I've seen has been just a little bit different. I've frequently worked on distributed teams across multiple time zones and locations. The physicality of gathering together isn't always feasible for a variety of reasons. Factor in multiple projects and timelines, other administrative and work-related tasks and meetings, and it's easy to see that getting everyone together at the same time can be really challenging.

The other reality is that I've witnessed design teams who really desire for critique to be ingrained into their process, and they want to hear and learn from their teammates. I've always felt that time zones shouldn't be a debilitating constraint—technology, along with a little bit of flexibility from a team, can be useful in getting past many of the obstacles that distributed teams face.

In light of the fact that many of us can't be in the same place to have that glorious-seeming ideal critique scenario, here's an approach I've worked with to get started with a distributed, fairly continuous critique system:

Define rules of critique

> The good news is that you've got a great book in your possession that provides you with all of the information that you need to do this.

Choose critique teams

> If you have a team of five people or fewer, you can lead the team in one-on-one critique sessions. If your team comprises six or more, you can share those duties with another member of your team. Consider rotating the role of the person leading critique sessions with some regularity to give everyone an opportunity. It's great to choose teams where people don't work on the same projects or products (if possible) and are in different physical locations.

Establish a critique operating rhythm

> This can be really simple—30-minute meetings, once a week, with a variety of approaches that can extend that into something more broad to help vary the types of critique you're receiving. Here are some examples of how a 12-week cycle might operate:

> - One-on-one meetings: 30-minute meetings between the critique leader and other members of the team.
>
> - Group critique meetings: Erica Deahl (*www.ericadeahl. com*) suggested that one-on-one critique sessions could be improved by adding group critique sessions, as well. Try rotating weeks between one-on-one meetings and group critique meetings to get the benefit from both types of sessions.
>
> - All design team meetings: In addition to the group critique meetings and the one-on-one meetings, consider a regular meeting with everyone across all teams. Allow team members to sign up to receive critique, and let everyone participate across your entire design practice. Youi could also expand this to include developers and/or other disciplines as it makes sense.

Your mileage may vary, of course, and you might (and I might, too!) find that a different approach works as you implement and gain feedback for your team. Use this framework as a way to kick off continuous critique for your team, and see where it leads.

By implementing continuous critique with the teams I've worked with (a relatively small investment, likely less than five percent of a team's utilization), I've seen several benefits, including:

- Identifies leaders and leadership in the team; everyone gets an opportunity to participate, lead, and offer improvements.

- Uncovers growth and training / learning needs; discussions across multiple projects and products help identify areas of growth needs for the team.

- Strengthens critique abilities across the team; it's being put into practice regularly and becomes embedded in the design culture.

- Increases distributed team communication, interaction, and engagement; team members who might not normally have reasons to interact get to spend time working together.

- Improves facilitation and presentation skills; the more we practice, the better we get at framing the scope of discussions and presenting our work.

- Improves design across the team; critique gives us opportunities to hear and learn from different perspectives and take action that makes our designs better.

FORMAL AND INFORMAL CRITIQUES

Standalone critiques themselves can take two forms: they can be formal, such as a scheduled meeting with a time, place, invites, and the whole 9 yards, or they can be as simple as asking someone for 10 minutes of her time to look over what we are working on—maybe chatting with someone over lunch, coffee, or drinks as we share our work and what we are trying to accomplish, and asking for her feedback.

Both formal and informal critiques are helpful. To ensure that we get the most out of them we need to consider the right type of critique setting for the situation.

Formal critiques provide a dedicated, predictable time, and as such, they typically give us an opportunity to collect a wider range of perspectives because we can gather more people.

Informal critiques provide designers with a way to quickly collect feedback and get answers to pressing questions so that they can continue working on their solutions instead of waiting for a scheduled meeting.

Organizations that have done well at integrating critique use both approaches and have constructed an environment in which both are not only accepted by team members, but expected.

Pixar, the animation powerhouse, uses a formal critique process as a way to analyze and strengthen works in progress while building collaboration. The practice, called "Dailies," is commonly used in television and film and is based on reviewing a previous day's footage to determine if reshoots and adjustments are needed. Seeing the potential and utility of this process, though, Pixar has adapted it such that it can improve and iterate on work at any stage, not just captured footage.

On a daily basis, Pixar staff from a variety of roles—whether it's writers, storyboard artists, character designers, directors, or whatever—will convene to examine and critique a work in progress. Making critique such a routine part of Pixar's process makes it possible for team members to build habits and "muscle memory" around productive conversations about their work. It also breaks down silos and provides a consistent opportunity to gain insights and perspectives about creations, allowing for continuous improvement. It's safe to assume that these Dailies are a contributing factor to the great work the Pixar team produces.

Whichever approach you choose, it is important to remember that the more you participate, the stronger your critique skills will become. As we said in Chapter 3, *practice, practice, practice!*

WHEN SHOULD YOU CRITIQUE?

A question that comes up often in our presentations and workshops is, "When should we be critiquing?"

Any time you're looking to take something you've done or created and improve upon it, you have an opportunity for critique. Although that's true in general, when we're talking about the practicalities and logistics of team collaboration and project timelines, the real answer becomes a bit more nuanced.

When thinking about what needs to be in place to critique an idea in a useful manner with respect to the idea itself, two very important considerations come up:

- We need to be able to clearly communicate the idea to others.

- We need to have the time to process the feedback we receive from the critique and use it to iterate on our idea.

Taking these things into consideration, we can place two points related to these considerations on a timeline that represents the life or "bakedness" of a design, as illustrated in Figure 4-1.

The Life of a Design

FIGURE 4-1
Timeline representation of the "life" of a design from initial idea to final product

Early critique

The leftmost end of the timeline represents the very first spark of an idea. At this point, things are very abstract and our own brains are still trying to make sense of the connections between aspects of the ideas that are coagulating in our minds. Think of it as the early embryonic stage of a baby's development (note I didn't say what kind of baby). It's just a lump. We still don't really know what it might be. Maybe it will have two arms, maybe eight. Or maybe it will have wings, and fangs, and shoot laser beams from its eyes and... well, you get the idea.

The gist is that at this early stage, we still need to develop our thoughts around the solution a bit more. If we tried to share them with others so that we could get their critique, we'd likely confuse the heck out of them because the idea itself isn't clear enough even to ourselves at this point. As soon as the first person asked us to clarify things, all we would be able to answer with is "I don't know."

To be able to critique, we first need to have enough of our own clarity around the idea so that we can clearly communicate it to others. This marks the first point that we can plot on the timeline, as depicted in Figure 4-2. Before it, critique is premature. It doesn't mean that we must wait until we've figured out every single detail and can thoroughly answer any question asked. In fact, at this early stage, there will still be a lot of details left to figure out and questions whose answers aren't known. That's alright.

The Life of a Design

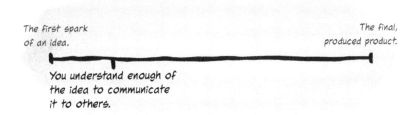

FIGURE 4-2

Plotting the point at which critique becomes effective during the "life" of a design"

Later critique

The rightmost side of the timeline represents the fully developed, or "fully baked," solution. At this point, whatever is going to be created has been. It's done. It's out in the world and it is what it is. Nothing more can be done to change it.

Those of us who work in digital products or services or who have any understanding of design philosophy recognize that this state is considered a fallacy. We can always learn from what we've created, iterate on our ideas, and release a *New! Improved! Design!*

Thinking in practical terms, specifically those of the design and production processes, we know that there is a point at which we have to let something go and allow it to be built with whatever details specified at that point in time. Then, we wait for the chance to work on it again and take it further—the next iteration or phase, if you will. There are processes and methodologies such as Lean and Agile that work to minimize the time between and maximize the frequency of iterations. But that point, that "time to let it go, even if just for a bit" is always there.

That point is the second point on the timeline (see Figure 4-3); it's the point at which we need to stop iterating for whatever amount of time, so that something can actually be produced. Often this point coincides with sign-offs, approvals, and design reviews (which we'll talk about in a bit).

The Life of a Design

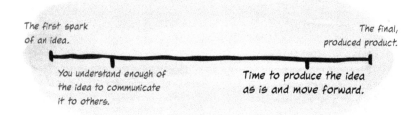

FIGURE 4-3

Plotting the point at which critique's effectiveness begins to diminish during the "life" of a design"

Finding the sweet spot

The space between the two points in Figure 4-3 is where critique is most immediately useful. Yes, it can be argued that we can still critique in the time to the right of the second point (we just need to wait until things circle back again before we can do something with the feedback). But here we're thinking about critique that is immediately useful; that is to say, the designer can walk away, think about the insights that were shared, and right away begin to iterate on the solution.

Now, the amount of time on either side of and between these two points will be highly dependent on any number of factors: the scale of the problems you're trying to solve, the scale of the idea itself, your team, your process and methods, and so on. We can't say that the first point comes exactly two days after the idea begins to form and then there's three weeks between when critique is useful and then another four days when it isn't.

Often these points are described in terms of percentages. For example, the best time to critique a solution is after it is 20 percent baked but before it's 80 percent baked. These kinds of labels can be useful in helping us to think and talk about when critique is useful, but they still have the possibility of being taken a bit too literally for our comfort. Instead, we think it's best to understand the dynamics and criteria we've described here and then use your judgment. In some cases, you'll get to that 20 percent mark very fast—maybe a matter of minutes or even seconds. Sometimes, it can take longer.

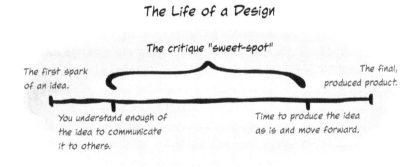

FIGURE 4-4

Identifying the critique sweet-spot during the "life" of a design"

Integrating Design Critique into the Lean Validation Cycle

Jeff Gothelf,
Principal, Neo

Within the cyclical, rapid pace of Agile projects, designs (and designers) can often become lost in the race to continue "feeding the Agile beast." This makes thoughtful reflection on the design even more difficult to achieve. Perhaps not surprisingly, it is exactly in these iterative environments that critique is most needed. In a recent engagement, we were helping an enterprise client conceive and then launch a new digital subscription business. In the conceptual stages of the project, designs were rough—often produced on nothing more than Sharpies and A4 paper—in an effort to bring alignment and team cohesion to the new product vision. Critique was rare; most conversations focused on workflow, customer needs, and integration into existing client and customer workflows.

With continued experimentation and testing, the team gained more certainty about the product's direction. With increased certainty comes increased fidelity. Our designer (the only one on the team at the time) was tasked with daily refinements of the interaction design as well as an ever-improving visual design. Week-long iterations, filled with continuous customer feedback and cadenced client reviews, allowed little time for design reflection of critique. Making things more challenging was the small size of our team: just four people made up of a product manager, two developers, and the designer. Our build/measure/learn cycle was the main source of design input.

Although the product features and workflow were improving on a weekly basis, there was a strong sense from the team that the design was stagnating. With engineers writing and refining features, the product manager liaising with client and customers, and the client scrambling to provide content on a timely basis, the challenge became pausing long enough for insightful design reflection to take place. In addition, we had the incremental challenge of integrating this new product into a suite of services and offerings of a client brand that had been around for decades. The design couldn't fall short.

Twelve weeks into this cycle the team realized that without meaningful design conversation, the product's success would be limited to early adopters and brand loyalists, not the broader new audience the client was seeking. With constant urging from the designer at first and the broader team second, the client finally agreed to add a designer. With the addition of this new team member, design responsibilities were now split between two people, making conversation possible at a tactical level between the two practitioners. In addition, this gave both designers the time they needed to be more thoughtful in their work and to seek out feedback both internally and from the client.

One of the first things to fall by the wayside in Lean validation work is design critique. This is natural because the refinement of the design is not essential if the product ideas are wrong. However, when product ideas, customer needs, and solution approaches gain traction, it's important to remember that great design differentiates products and focus needs to be shifted to this work. Adequately integrating critique into a Lean or Agile environment requires a few things:

Ensure that designers aren't limited in their ability to seek out critique
> Tasking one designer with interaction design, visual design, content, research, and frontend coding limits that person's ability to seek out and incorporate meaningful feedback into their design work. It's important to add designers on to the team to help distribute workload, provide practitioner-level critique, and ensure design details aren't being missed.

Set expectations about when and how frequently critiques will occur
> There is a tough balance to maintain between clients who love seeing (and can easily react to) design work and the need to validate early product ideas. Set client expectations that design critique meetings will begin at some point during the project and will become increasingly frequent as features mature and customer feedback increases.

Keep discussions broad at first
> Design critique sessions early in the Lean validation process can sometimes prove too tactical yet need to be brought back in as soon as product ideas reach a threshold of market validation. Keep critique sessions focused starting initially with a style guide–level critique targeting product-wide elements and then digging into tactical critiques that look at unique elements and implementations across the product suite.

Agile processes are iterative. Design processes are also iterative. Their natural integration is not only inevitable, it's tailor-made. Just as code is reviewed regularly in these processes, design critique must also become commonplace. The techniques shared provide a framework for starting the Agile critique initiative. As with any process, the recommendations are just that, starting points. Pay attention to the unique needs of your organization and adjust these frameworks to reflect your industry and culture's unique needs.

HOW OFTEN SHOULD YOU CRITIQUE?

Early on in our exploration into critique, Aaron and I were asked by an audience member at one of our talks if there is such a thing as "too much critique."

I (Adam), in a bit of zealotry and over-enthusiasm replied, "No. Not at all!" And then I went on and on about how critique was the best thing to ever happen to modern civilization. Well, not really... but you get the picture.

We wish we could find that audience member and apologize.

Having had much more time to work with different teams and organizations as well as listen to the experiences of many, many people, we agree that yes, there is absolutely such a thing as too much critique. As with timing though, there isn't a specific number or formula that indicates exactly how much is too much. Instead, it's an innate sense or sensitivity that a team or individuals develop over time as their skills and comfort with critique improve. It's the sense that critiques are no longer helping or contributing to the momentum of the solution or the project; instead, they are possibly inhibiting it.

There might be too much critique when the team begins to sense that the amount of advancement between critiques is so small that it makes it feel as though progress has stalled. Or, perhaps when critiques are just talking in circles and the changes being made as a result of the insights collected in those discussions aren't doing anything to advance the design, it might be the case that there is too much critique or it is happening too often.

Or relatedly, if members of the team feel that critique—more specifically formal critiques—are being required so frequently that they can't push the design forward enough between them, there might be too much critique.

Additionally, if critiques begin to be seen or used by team members as a validation mechanism because there isn't enough confidence in their ideas either by the team or the designer themselves, there might be too much critique.

Answering the question of how often to critique is too nebulous to take on. Your needs will be different depending on the individuals and team. Given the scale of what you're looking for feedback on, sometimes you'll want critique very frequently, sometimes not so much. With practice, you'll know when the time is appropriate.

The key is honing that sense of when it's right and when it's too much, and that only comes with practice. Be flexible. As you try incorporating critique at various points and times and frequencies, think about whether it feels like too much or too little. Talk with other members of the team and get their perspectives. Adjust your timing and try some more.

WHAT SHOULD YOU CRITIQUE?

Another common question that Aaron and I hear is, "What should we be critiquing? Sketches? Wireframes? Visual Design Comps? Prototypes?"

The answer is, yes, all those and more.

Anything you want to improve can be critiqued. The documents listed above (sketches, wireframes, and so on) are all representations of a solution. The form of documentation doesn't matter. If you're looking to iterate and improve the solution, critique it. Going further, it isn't just the design we create for our project that we can critique. We can critique any and all of the artifacts we create: personas, scenarios, journey maps, whatever. We can critique the tools, methodologies, processes, and so on that we use. We can critique it all. We really can... Critique. All. The. Things.

But what changes when you go from critiquing a wireframe to a visual design mockup? Or how about design principles? What's different when you're critiquing those?

No matter what you're critiquing, the framework stays the same. What are the objectives? What elements or aspects of the product relate to those objectives? Are those aspects or elements effective? Why or why not?

What changes when critiquing different artifacts or design elements are the objectives against which you're analyzing. The objectives for the product will carry through in critiques of any and all aspects of the design, but some will be more pertinent at times, depending on what you're analyzing. For example, the color pallet you choose might or might not be relevant to a goal of increasing authenticated visits to your website or reducing calls to the support desk.

Different aspects of the design can also have their own unique objectives. Often, we see these in the form of principles and best practices. A team might establish principles that are specific to interaction design or some specific to visual design. Each of these, in turn, has its own best practices that should be considered.

This extends beyond the design to anything else you might critique, too. For example, if a team is working on establishing design principles, what it comes up with could (and should) be critiqued against best practices for creating design principles.

So, regardless of what's being critiqued, the structure of the conversation doesn't really change. What does change is that against which the object being critiqued is being analyzed.

Central Idea

Standalone critiques, whether they're formal meetings or casual discussions, are a great way to incorporate critique because of the flexibility they offer around when and how teams can use them.

Collaborative Activities

As design practices mature within individuals and organizations, collaborative activities are playing a larger role in the process. Often referred to as workshops or working sessions, these activities pull together multiple people to work on solving a problem simultaneously and collectively.

Because of their usefulness as both an iteration driver and as a consensus builder (see Chapter 1), critique can be a powerful activity to incorporate into collaborative activities.

ENTER THE BRAINSTORM

One of the most common "activities" in a workshop is the *brainstorm*. The idea behind brainstorms is that, as a group, people can come up with more potential solutions to a challenge than if they worked individually.

Although it's a nice idea, we can't say that we've often seen it work out that way. Instead, what we commonly see in brainstorms, following a presentation of the challenge to be solved, is a period of silence. Then, one person proposes an idea. Other participants then begin to analyze the idea and discuss why it might or might not work, while the remainder of the team is trying to come up with their own ideas. Then, someone else proposes a second idea. That idea might be completely new, but it's more than likely that it's a variation on the previous idea. The discussion picks up again, now analyzing both presented ideas, and this pattern repeats one or two more times. It's rare that we've seen brainstorms executed this way produce more than a handful of unique ideas.

The problems with brainstorms as they're commonly executed are many.

Brainstorms lack focus

In many of the brainstorms we've observed the challenge to be solved has not been adequately defined or broken apart to allow people to come up with ideas. Often it can feel like someone on the team encountered a problem, determined she couldn't or shouldn't solve it on her own, and so dropped everything to call everyone together in the hopes that magically after a few hours they'd have a solution.

Brainstorms lack structure and facilitation

Coordinating the mental processes of a group of individuals isn't easy, but it's essential to productive collaborative activities. When everyone is working in different directions, it can be impossible to resolve questions and find agreements.

Brainstorms devolve quickly into design-by-committee

Often, because of the limited ideas, lack of structure, and pressure to have a solution at the end of the session, brainstorms often shift to a goal of getting everyone in a room to say yes to a solution without much regard as to whether it's the right solution.

Now, this doesn't mean that brainstorms are bad and should be avoided. Harnessing the power of a group and the fact that you have many minds working on a challenge in order to find as many solutions as possible is a worthy and righteous goal. A good idea can come from anywhere and the best way to find great ideas is to have lots of ideas.

However, we need to put some thought into how we go about planning and running brainstorms. Let's take a look at a very simple framework that can instantly improve the quantity and quality of ideas your team conceives.

BUILDING BETTER BRAINSTORMS

Let's think about the objectives of the average brainstorm. Of course, the primary objective is to come up with lots of ideas—as many as possible. But more often than not, we also have the objective of figuring out which one of the ideas the team should pursue. And if we're doing things right that idea should be the one the team feels most works toward the goals we're trying to achieve.

With those objectives in mind, let's take them one by one.

Generate as many ideas as possible

Why is it that brainstorms often struggle to generate more than a handful of ideas? The answer is simple, and it's a phrase we've used quite a few times already, though not in reference to an obstacle: critical thinking.

Critical thinking is the nemesis of creative or generative thinking. With critical thinking we're trying to determine if an idea will or won't do what we want it to. The problem with most brainstorms is that we're not doing anything to prevent participants from thinking critically. So, not only are some participants spending their time and energy thinking about the ideas that have been presented—meaning they aren't coming up with more ideas—but other participants who might be coming up with ideas aren't sharing them because as they're coming up with them, they're analyzing them prematurely. Thus the group that's formulating new ideas determines that they aren't worth mentioning and keeps those ideas to themselves. This is exactly what we don't want to happen!

Additionally challenging to coming up with lots of ideas in a brainstorm is the way in which participants are pushed to interact and discuss things almost immediately after being presented with the challenge to be solved. This means that before an individual is even able to form his own perspective on the challenge and possible solutions, he's forced to listen to, make sense of, and discuss the perspectives of others. It's pretty hard to come up with ideas when all that's going on.

To generate lots of ideas, we need to utilize activities that minimize or remove the opportunity for critical thinking and give individual participants an opportunity to form their own perspective. These kinds of activities are called *divergent thinking activities*. These are activities that push participants to consider lots of possibilities without consideration of their validity. How do they remove or minimize critical thinking? Well, sometimes it's just a matter of a good facilitator watching out for it, but more often than not, these activities involve some kind of time limit and a challenge. For example: sketch six to eight ideas for this interface in five minutes.

OK. On to our second objective.

Determine which idea to pursue

This one isn't so difficult. As we mentioned, most brainstorms do already do this, just badly. If we began our brainstorm with divergent thinking activities, the activities we want to do here are convergent thinking activities. These are activities that push participants to compare, contrast, consolidate, and eliminate ideas. This is where participants come together to discuss ideas and collaboratively determine what to do with them. At the end of this process, by virtue of consolidating and eliminating ideas, we're left with far fewer solutions than we started with.

Which leads us to the final objective.

Ensure that the idea(s) you're left with are the strongest ones

Consolidating similar ideas only goes so far in shrinking our pool of possible solutions. Elimination, or more specifically, deciding which ideas not to pursue, is really the key to figuring out what we're going to pursue. Some ideas will be easy to eliminate; they might be cost or time prohibitive, or maybe they involve acquiring the magical horn of the last purple unicorn from the far-away land of Trilandia. But what about the rest?

Voting is a common mechanism used to determine which ideas should stay in the fight. Participants vote on the idea or ideas they think are strongest. But it's more than likely that the criteria each participant is using for making that decision varies and might or might not have much to do with the goals of the project.

Enter critique

By incorporating critique as a precursor to voting or a voting-like activity, we prime the pump, so to speak. We get participants thinking about the ideas that have been presented through the lens of the agreed-upon objectives for the product. By way of conversation, we've likely already begun to see where consensus lies with regard to which ideas are strongest relative to the objectives, even before the vote takes place.

Taken all together, these considerations give us a very simple framework for our brainstorms, which you can see in Figure 4-5:

1. Divide your time into two main phases.

2. In the first phase, utilize divergent thinking activities with which you can generate a large number of possible solutions without concern about their validity or quality.

3. In the second phase, plan for convergent activities that push participants to examine the proposed ideas, looking for ways to categorize, consolidate, and eliminate ideas.

4. Incorporate critique as part of the second phase to ensure that ideas are being kept or eliminated based on their strengths with respect to the product's objectives.

Central Idea

Critique provides a powerful mechanism to help teams make choices that are focused on product objectives during collaborative activities such as brainstorms.

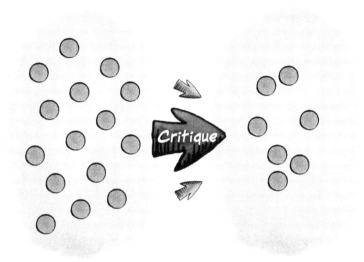

Divergent Thinking
Activities that push participants to generate multiple solutions to a challenge by minimizing their ability to think critically.

Convergent Thinking
Activities in which participants compare, contrast, consolidate, and eliminate ideas based on some set of criteria.

FIGURE 4-5
The basic structure of a "brainstorm" workshop using divergent and convergent activities with critique as a transitional mechanism between them

AN EXAMPLE: DESIGN STUDIO

Adam and I are big fans of the Design Studio methodology. Design Studio is a perfect example of the framework we just mentioned in action. The technique itself is based upon architecture, industrial design, and some art schools where "studio" is the core component of the curriculum. Studio classes follow a basic iterative structure in which students are presented with a challenge, asked to generate a number of possible solutions, and then present those solutions to the instructor and class for critique. Based on that critique, the students then go back and refine a subset of their ideas, to be presented and critiqued again. This pattern repeats until an end solution is determined and continually refined.

The methodology was adapted to digital design practices and popularized by Todd Zaki Warfel in many presentations; it is noted in his book, *Prototyping: A Practitioner's Guide* (Rosenfeld Media, 2009).

Although there are many variations on the methodology, there are a few core criteria that remain consistent:

- The order of activities within one phase, called a *charrette*, of a studio is always sketch > present > critique.

- There are at least two charrettes. Three is a more commonly used number.

- The first charrette is always individuals sketching their own ideas for the given challenge.

Adam and I have been using Design Studio with our teams and clients for years now and have had a lot success using it to get teams to collaboratively work to define interfaces for apps, websites, and other products. What follows is the setup we've developed and refined over the years.

We use a three-charrette model. Each charrette has a set time that allows for sketching concepts, presenting them to other participants, and receiving critique. Participants are broken up into teams of no more than six individuals. If there are not six participants to a team that is OK. Ideally, three to six participants works well for the exercises. Teams are constructed so that to the degree possible they are cross-functional; that is, we don't have one team comprised completely of designers and one entirely of developers. A facilitator (or two) helps keep time for the exercises, ensures the meeting stays on track, and remains available for questions.

Preparation

Participants should be equipped with the problem statement for the product they'll be designing. They should also be given the product's business goals, scenarios, personas, and any other previously agreed-upon artifacts that will provide the context needed for their designs. It is very helpful to the participants if they aren't seeing these items for the first time, so we work to get them distributed before the session.

It's also important to have the right tools ready. You can find almost all of these tools at an office supply store and they are relatively inexpensive. Here's what we typically use (see also Figure 4-6):

FIGURE 4-6
Common supplies used in a Design Studio activity

- A timer for time-boxing each charrette. Time-boxing is nothing more than putting a limit on the amount of time for an activity.

- Paper for sketching. We use two kinds, 6-ups and 1-ups. Don't get put off by the names; it's just grid paper. 6-ups are pages broken down into six small grids, and 1-ups are one large grid. Really, any paper will do, but we use these because the smaller spaces on 6-ups used in early charrettes restrict participants from including too much detail.

- Black markers for sketching. We don't let participants use pencil— having the ability to erase can slow people down. Also, because markers draw thicker lines, they prevent people from getting too detailed.

- Red and green pens for the critique sessions. During critique, you can use green pens to mark the elements of a design that are considered particularly strong, or those that could be strong with more work. Use the red pens to mark elements that are considered ineffective or provide little value toward the product's objectives.

- Painters tape to post sketches to the wall during critiques. Posting to the wall requires the designer to stand with his team. At times, we've noticed that in presentations designers will hold up their sketches and stand behind them as if they're some sort of barrier between themselves and the rest of the team. Taping things up to the wall eliminates this.

The activity

The format of charrettes is as follows (see also Figure 4-7):

Charrette 1

Participants are given eight minutes to sketch as many concepts as they can come up with using the 6-up paper.

The goal of this round is for the participants to generate as many ideas as possible without over thinking things. Often, we'll challenge participants to see if they can come up with at least five ideas.

When the time is up, participants post their sketches on the wall, present their ideas to their teammates (three minutes), and receive critique on them (four to five minutes).

Charrette 2

Participants take the feedback they heard during their critiques as well as the ideas and feedback that they heard their teammates present and receive and revisit their sketches. The participants now have eight minutes to iterate on their previous sketches and come up with a singular concept, again using 6-up paper. This allows individuals to form their own conclusions based on the strongest ideas that came up during the critiques as well as go a bit deeper into details.

When the eight minutes are up, the team tapes their sketches to the wall and again presents their concepts and receives critique. Just like in the first round, the participants get three minutes to present their sketches and receive critique from their team for four to five minutes.

Participants are given 20 minutes to work collaboratively within their teams to come up with a singular design concept based on the critique they received in the last two rounds. By doing this, the teams work together to get a better understanding of how groups compromise and where consensus has been achieved.

When the time is up, teams present their concepts to the other teams to receive critique. The teams each have three minutes to present their ideas and seven minutes to receive critique from the other teams.

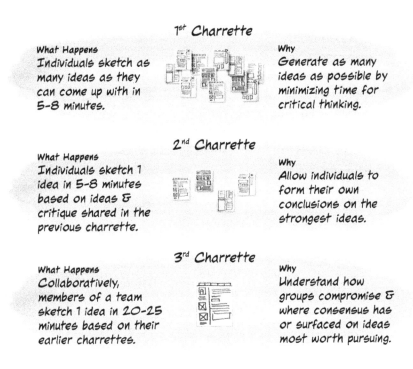

1ˢᵗ Charrette

What Happens
Individuals sketch as many ideas as they can come up with in 5-8 minutes.

Why
Generate as many ideas as possible by minimizing time for critical thinking.

2ⁿᵈ Charrette

What Happens
Individuals sketch 1 idea in 5-8 minutes based on ideas & critique shared in the previous charrette.

Why
Allow individuals to form their own conclusions on the strongest ideas.

3ʳᵈ Charrette

What Happens
Collaboratively, members of a team sketch 1 idea in 20-25 minutes based on their earlier charrettes.

Why
Understand how groups compromise & where consensus has or surfaced on ideas most worth pursuing.

FIGURE 4-7
An overview of the 3 charrette model for a Design Studio activity

The aftermath

With the studio just about complete, we now have multiple concepts that are based on the ideas, critique, and compromise of each team. We next have participants talk about any common themes or patterns that emerged, making sure to document and share any open questions or assumptions that need to be validated.

It's important to note that for most situations, we do not recommend using a studio to generate a single ultimate solution. In many cases, it's unlikely that all of the considerations that need to be taken into account to determine a single solution can be addressed in the time constraints of a studio activity. Instead, as we use it, following the studio, the design team takes the ideas from the final charrette and works to create a single solution taking into account further analysis, critique, and other considerations and dependencies.

WHEN NOT TO USE DESIGN STUDIO

Design Studio is a great technique for quick collaboration, helping a team find consensus, and begin to see the direction that their design will take. But like any tool, it isn't the best fit for every situation. Depending on your circumstances your project may not yet be in a position to utilize Design Studio or there may be circumstances that require you to rethink aspects of Design Studio or pursue a different approach all together. For example:

The problem hasn't been framed adequately

If the problem hasn't been adequately framed, there isn't enough context and definition to guide the team in generating ideas. Participants are left to generate ideas based on their individual understanding of the problem that is being solved. And they may struggle to generate any ideas because the lack of framing leaves the problem too nebulous with too many potential solutions to explore.

The problem has been framed, but there is no agreement on the framing

In some cases, we find that a portion of the team, perhaps the designers or researchers, has worked to frame the problem, but that framing hasn't yet been shared, understood and agreed upon by the team. This can often derail a Design Studio because, rather than generate ideas, the group will instead become mired in discussion and debate about what the framing should be. This is of course, an important discussion to be had, but if this discussion starts when you're trying to kick off a Design Studio, it means that the group isn't ready and you should have had this conversation earlier.

Alternatively, if you are able to get participants into the sketching phase of a studio without agreed upon framing, participants will generate ideas based on their own opinion of what the problem is, rather than a shared framing. This causes complications during the critiques and iterations in a studio because people are analyzing and judging the value of ideas on different sets of criteria.

A concept already exists from which the team can't or won't stray

Design Studio pushes participants to consider as many possibilities as they can come up with. This means that the ideas that emerge at the end of a studio may look very different than an existing design or product that the team already has. In order for Design Studios to be effective, the participants (and leadership) need to be OK with that. If the team has been instructed to make minimal changes to an existing design, then chances are they'll struggle throughout a studio activity and with determining what to do with the ideas that arise from it.

The team is not open to using Design Studio

Design Studios require active participation. Everyone involved will be sketching, presenting and sharing their ideas. As such, participants need to approach the activity with attitudes that support it.

Some people just won't have an attitude that fits. Some will hate the idea of having to share their ideas. Some will hate the pressure of being asked to come up with solutions. Some just won't want to participate at all. In these situations it's worth it to at least try to get people involved, but if they repeatedly resist, it is not worth forcing the issue.

Overly complicated remote situations

Design Studio is best executed in person; for this activity, there is nothing like collaborating and working together face to face. With that said, remote Design Studio can work (we both do them regularly with our teams) as long as expectations are clear from the beginning, teams are equipped with tools like document cameras, and a solid Internet connection is available. Things get difficult when participants experience connection issues, or when a participant is working from an environment with lots of background activity and distractions.

Another instance in which you might want to consider alternative techniques, is when you have unbalanced remote distribution of your participants. For example, if all but one person is located in one place, so everyone is working face to face except for the sole remote participant, it can become a bit difficult to work, particularly with respect to the group components of a studio. Or, if all your designers are in one location and your developers in another, it can be difficult because you don't want your teams to be constructed entirely of people within the same role. The key is to think through how you'll form your teams and how the people on those teams will interact and contribute. If you can figure out something that will work, you can probably pull off a remote studio. One common fall back for situations like this is to, regardless of who happens to be in the same location, have everyone participate virtually.

Conducting Design Reviews

Whereas standalone critiques and collaborative activities are great and recommended ways to incorporate critique into the design process, design reviews are a bit different.

Design reviews are a common type of meeting that we find in projects in most organizations. Sometimes they have different names. To clarify what we're referring to, these meetings share the following characteristics:

- They are generally meetings held toward the end of the design phase.

- They include a goal of collecting approval from someone on the design thus far so that efforts can shift to some new focus—the design of a different set of functionality, a shift in process to development, and so on.

- If approval is not captured, these meetings focus on identifying the changes that need to be made to obtain approval in the future.

Regardless of what they're called, these meetings can be seen as a form of "gate," something that the design and team needs to pass through in order to proceed to something else.

Because a design—and changes to it—is being discussed in these sessions, they are often where teams we've worked with expect critique to be happening. However, even though feedback is a part of design reviews, they are not the same as critiques. The goals and logistics of these sessions in many cases make design reviews challenging for critique.

THE CHALLENGES DESIGN REVIEWS POSE TO CRITIQUE

Their intended outcome is approval

As previously mentioned, these sessions are typically held for the purpose of getting an approval or sign-off of some kind, an agreement that it's OK to shift the focus of work onto something else.

Even though their main activity is discussion of the design, the objective of these discussions is very different from those of a critique. Critiques are held with the intention of iterating on the design. It is understood and expected by all those involved that the design will be worked on further. The critique discussion is a tool used to inform where and how it might be iterated upon.

Specific changes are given as feedback

Because of this difference in objectives, in instances where approval isn't received in design reviews, the feedback collected is often in the form of a list of what needs to change or be improved in the design. The thinking here is along the lines of, "It isn't ready yet, but if you do these things and show it to us again, we'll give you the OK."

As we've shared in earlier chapters, though, critique isn't about problem solving and specifying solutions. This is directive feedback and it is problematic to critique for a number of reasons.

Too many people and people with the wrong intentions are involved

The majority of the people we find in these meetings are there to ensure that their own list of interests and requirements are present in the final design, not necessarily comparing the design to its objectives to determine what might or might not be effective. When this is the setting, motives are skewed and goals are much different than in a normal critique session.

Additionally, because design reviews are usually to get approval, the group in the meeting is often too large to have productive conversations. Adam was once involved in a design review with more than 70 people in attendance, most by phone. How is it possible to have a productive, coherent conversation with that many people all trying to make sure their voice is heard?

Design review timing is determined by the project's timeline

The timing of design reviews is usually determined by a project's timeline and often held toward the end of a design phase or release cycle. Not only does this timing impede a team's ability to collect and make use of critique because there isn't enough time following the review to fully utilize it, but it is completely disjointed from when a team might actually need critique.

We should be able to conduct critiques whenever it's useful for designers to understand the impact or effect of the choices they've made so far in order to iterate further on their creations. This typically means that effective critiques can begin fairly early in the design process and are held numerous times throughout.

ADDRESSING THE CHALLENGES OF DESIGN REVIEWS

None of this is to say that design reviews aren't a necessity. For some organizations, the need to gather everyone and collect approvals or sign-off is going to be essential. And, even though the intention behind critique differs from design reviews, the utility of the techniques we share in this book is to make feedback more useful in informing design decisions. If you've found these meetings and the feedback collected from them to be challenging, using techniques for gathering and facilitating critique can go a long way to making them better.

Specifically, to address the challenges design reviews present, we recommend the following to help prepare and get the most out of them.

Take control of the review

This doesn't mean that you need to hijack the meeting, per se, but try to get into as much of a lead role as possible. If you can be the one to set up and organize the meeting, do it. If you can be the one to lead and facilitate the meeting, do it. This way you have an opportunity to work toward steering discussions so that they focus on comparing the design to its objectives, not just whether it has approval. This will give you the opportunity to measure the feedback against the goals and the intended outcomes, and in so doing, help in getting actionable feedback.

Recap the objectives

To the degree you're able to, remind people of the agreed upon objectives for the design. If you're leading or facilitating the meeting, review these at the beginning of the session. If not, when you have a chance to speak try to bring them up. By reminding the team of the objectives for the project, you can inform their thinking so that it stays closer to the intent of critique.

Use the techniques we suggest for dealing with difficult people

In Chapter 6, we cover techniques for handling situations that involve people behaving in a difficult manner during a critique. It's inevitable that you'll encounter them. In many situations, the behaviors exhibited by participants in a design review are very similar to those situations. Techniques such as direct inquiry and *laddering* as well as strong facilitation skills go a long way toward getting better, more useful feedback out of design reviews.

Do not rely on design reviews for critique

We should not rely on design reviews as the only form of critique. If we are regularly critiquing before and leading up to a design review, the review can serve its purpose. It can act as a focused forum for approval of designs. Additionally, the team will have established a shared understanding about the goals and progress of the designs leading to a more focused review with fewer personal agendas.

Central Idea

Design reviews present challenges to the core intention of critique: continuous improvement. But, because the techniques used in critique work to make feedback more useful in the design process, they can be used to improve feedback gathered during design reviews.

Wrapping Up

Critique's primary utility is as an iteration driver. There are many, many opportunities for it to occur within our practice. Whenever we are looking to improve or iterate on an idea or process, or almost anything, we have an opportunity for critique.

There are three points within the design process that present opportunities for incorporating critique.

- **Standalone critiques (both formal and informal or ad hoc):** These are meetings or discussions with the solitary purpose of critiquing a creation so that it can be iterated upon further.

- **Collaborative activities:** Activities that bring team members together to work on idea generation and selection. Including critique in these activities helps teams identify where there is consensus around ideas with the most value to the product's objectives.

- **Design reviews:** Meetings that include some intention to collect sign-off or approval on a design. Although we recommend that these be handled separate from critiques, as feedback is collected during reviews, we can use many of the tools and techniques for critique to make the feedback collected as useful as possible.

No matter how you incorporate critique it's important to remember the following:

- **Start small.** The more people involved in a conversation, the more difficult it is to manage. When introducing or practicing critique, start with small groups or just pairs and build from there.

- **Think before you speak.** Listening is paramount. How can you offer good feedback or act on the feedback you've received if you don't accurately understand what you're being told?

- **Choose participants carefully.** Critique is not for everyone. Some people struggle more than others. To the degree you can, think about how you put people together to best improve their skills and comfort level.

[5]

Facilitating Critique

We've described what goes into critique, the aspects of organizational culture that support it, and how critique fits within the design process. What about the conversations themselves? How can we make critique discussions go smoothly?

Facilitation is often seen as a tool for getting meetings or projects that have gotten out of hand back on track. But in reality, it has a much wider application.

Facilitation is the conscious, balanced management of conversations toward a conclusion. It begins with an understanding of the objectives and purpose of a discussion. It then works to ensure that those objectives are met through measures that ask appropriate questions, ensure shared understanding, and allow participants to provide their perspectives to the group. It's a valuable skill that helps guide our conversations.

Because the best critiques are a dialogue, we can view facilitation as a vital component of the critique process. Without it, our critiques can become unruly, with participants analyzing different aspects of the design against their own criteria. Even though some of this analysis can turn out to be relevant and useful, a significant portion of it will not. And the inconsistent and sporadic nature of its delivery, due to the lack of structure, can make it difficult to follow and discern what is useful and what isn't, which ultimately impacts the decisions we make in our designs.

Through facilitation, we can provide structures with which people can share their individual thoughts. We can help ensure that participants maintain focus on the objectives of the design and keep in scope with regard to which aspects of the design are being discussed at any point in the conversation.

Chapter 2 discusses a basic framework or flow for critique, which you can see in Figure 5-1. This structure provides us with the flow we want to produce in our conversations using various facilitation methods as applicable.

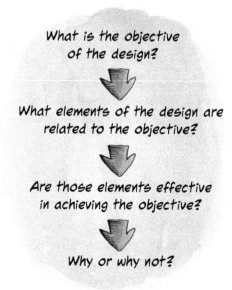

FIGURE 5-1
The four questions that comprise the basic critique framework

Now, let's talk about some of the rules, techniques, and other things to keep in mind as we work to focus our feedback discussions and make them more effective. Although what we'll cover in this chapter is written from the perspective of facilitating formal critiques, namely meetings set up specifically for critique, or for which critique is a significant item on the agenda, much of it also applies to casual, informal discussions, as well. Facilitation isn't always a formal role. Sometimes it's just a matter of the questions you choose to ask and how you choose to ask them."

Central Idea

Facilitation is an invaluable skill when it comes to gathering useful critique. Strong facilitation keeps critique conversations focused and productive.

Understanding the Rules of Critique

There are four key rules that we need to keep in mind. Paying attention to these rules will help to ensure that our discussion remains focused, efficient, and effective. It's the facilitator's job to make certain these rules are adhered to, but it's a good idea to share them with the team.

Especially in formal critiques, we want to confirm that all participants know about and understand these rules. Don't hesitate to review them quickly at the beginning of the discussion or post them in the room where the critique is being conducted.

EVERYONE IS EQUAL

Organizational hierarchy has an uncanny ability to make people feel like their perspectives and opinions carry more or less weight than others. Although it's true that an organization might make decisions based on what its leaders think as opposed to other employees, it isn't inherently true that their opinions are more accurate just because they're executives.

It is important in a critique that we remember this and that everyone's observations and perspectives are listened to equally. More attention should not be paid to those of a higher position just because of that position. You may be familiar with the acronym HiPPO (Highest Paid Person's Opinion); it's a killer when it comes to effective critique.

Moreover, the contributors themselves should feel like, and see others as, equal contributors. They should recognize that their feedback is just as valued as that of everyone else, regardless of their job title. Useful insights can come from anyone and, if participants are sensing an inequality, they might be hesitant to share their feedback. Or, they might decide to just go along with the feedback expressed by someone else instead of voicing their own perspectives. When this happens, we can miss out on valuable information.

Think about your team or the people you'll be pulling together for the critique and see if you can, from past experience, sense how much of an issue this will be. Consider talking to the group about this rule and others beforehand. We've even had success in some situations talking directly with the team members and executives whose opinions are being catered to about the issue and gotten their help in addressing the issue. Remember, it isn't the case that everyone in this position wants this kind of behavior. Many of the executives we've worked with have recognized the negative effect it can have on a team and their work and have taken steps to address it.

During a session, if you notice that people are being quiet because of a "superior's" participation, ask for feedback directly from those people. Or, if someone is throwing their weight around with their opinions, consider talking to them about it, perhaps after the meeting to avoid it happening again in the future. To address the inequality seen in critiques he's run, Adam has even called breaks during which he's raised concerns to the organization leaders in attendance.

If we begin with a level playing field, when it comes time to make decisions on how to iterate and develop our designs, we can ensure that we are able to hear perspectives from across the team. And later, as we review the feedback collected, we can take into consideration an individual's expertise and experience, and not focus solely on her position in the hierarchy.

Eliminating the influence of organizational hierarchy can be a tough rule to implement depending on the culture of a team or organization. But for critique to be successful, it is a key element. Remember that critique is not direction. Even though it's true that in many organizations a director, executive, or other leader's decisions will take priority over the thoughts of others, we want to keep that separate, and hopefully after a critique. Part of what we want to reveal in the critique is a variety of perspectives from different areas of expertise so that any decisions made later are as well informed as they can be.

EVERYONE IS A CRITIC

Everyone in the critique session should participate. Some individuals might be intimidated or won't feel like they have anything of value to contribute because they aren't a designer. Or, they might just not feel comfortable saying things that they fear will make the designer feel bad. But as we mentioned in the previous rule, great insights can come from anyone, and we can miss out on helpful information when people do not participate in critiques.

Ensuring that everyone participates also helps prevent situations in which an individual might not say much during the critique but ends up expressing any concerns he had after the fact, when it is often too late to act on those concerns.

AVOID PROBLEM SOLVING

This can be the hardest of all the rules. Avoiding problem solving can be tough. We do it instinctively. It is a natural inclination for many of us to come up with solutions as soon as we perceive a problem or inefficiency.

To understand why this is problematic in critique, we need to remember that the human brain does not consciously think both analytically (taking in and comparing information) and creatively (generating possible solutions by combining ideas [otherwise known as problem solving]) simultaneously. This process of multitasking instead forces our brain to divide resources between the two processes and then actively switch between them.

In earlier chapters we described the toggle our brains make between creative and analytical thinking while we're working. It happens so frequently that we often aren't even aware it's happening. It can take a lot of practice and skill to keep our brains from bouncing back and forth, and to remain focused on just one process.

When an individual in a critique begins proposing a new solution or a change, it means that she's switched mindsets. Her brain has toggled from analytical thinking to creative thinking.

Now think about this toggle happening independently within every participant in a critique. You can begin to see why it's problematic. When new ideas start being proposed, you have some folks in the critique who are in a creative mental process, some in an analytical one (still analyzing the original design), some analyzing the new idea, and some in a third process: comprehension (trying to just understand the new idea).

More than likely, some people's brains are jumping from one process to another. A big challenge in facilitating any discussion, not just critiques, is keeping everyone focused on the same objective. In the case of a critique, that objective is analysis of the design being presented. When problem solving begins to happen, the coordination becomes lost and everyone heads in different mental directions.

On top of that, problem solving can derail the session by not allowing session goals to be met due to the focus switching to solving a specific issue seen in the design rather than analyzing the aspects for which we were looking to collect insights. If we have five items to review and critique in the meeting and we veer off to problem solving while looking at item number two, the chances are that we'll never make it to item number three, never mind five.

But it's too damned difficult to *not* solve problems.

The tendency to generate ideas for solutions can be instinctual and unconscious. You've probably seen this yourself in one form or another. It's not uncommon during a usability test, or in any environment really, to hear someone encountering an issue say something like, "they really should…" or "it would be better if they…" before ever articulating the problem he's trying to solve.

If that's the case, how can we expect to prevent a room full of people from doing it when we ask them to analyze our designs?

Well, we can't.

What's important here is to understand why the problem solving is happening and the impact it can have on the remainder of the discussion.

If someone has jumped to a solution without describing the issue in the design that she's trying to solve, ask questions that work toward identifying what that issue is and how it relates to the objectives of the design.

If someone is spending a lot of time trying to describe his new solution to you, and you understand the issue or insight he's trying to raise, work toward getting him to hold onto that idea for a future discussion that will be focused on exploration so that you can continue with the analysis as planned, as depicted in Figure 5-2.

Here's another possibility: if everyone gets really hung up on a specific issue with the design and can't avoid trying to solve it, or perhaps the impact of how it might be solved is so huge that it brings further critique of the current into question, try pausing or postponing the remainder of the critique and switch right then to exploring solutions.

What is paramount is to keep everyone in the same mental process.

FIGURE 5-2
Demonstration of postponing idea exploration until after a critique

DON'T RUSH TO MAKE DECISIONS ON THE CHANGES TO BE MADE

The output of a critique is not a list of specific changes for the designer to go back and make. Instead, the desired output is a set of new observations and understandings about the design and whether it is meeting the objectives set for it. This goes back to the previous rule. If a list of changes is coming out of a critique session, problem solving is taking the place of analysis.

After a critique should come a period of exploration, using the new insights to frame challenges and generate possible solutions. For some of the insights uncovered during a critique, the changes to be made will be small and obvious, but for many there is the potential for numerous solutions to be thought of and we should give ourselves time to do this. If we rush to make all of the decisions on changes to be made while we're still trying to analyze things in our critique, it's likely that we'll miss opportunities for stronger ideas or make premature decisions that cause more problems down the road. This is another rule that might raise some eyebrows when sharing it with your team.

Waiting to make decisions affords the designer time to digest all of the feedback she received during the session. She can examine it in light of the goals, principles, scenarios, and personas of the project. The designer can then follow up with individuals or the entire group about specific points of feedback and continue the discussion, idea generation, and exploration.

The "I Like..." or "I Don't Like..." Rule

Often, when we talk about the rules of critique we are asked about the rule of thumb on avoiding the use of the phrases "I like..." or "I don't like...." The thinking behind this rule is that critique itself isn't about what the individual likes or dislikes; that likely is not relevant to whether the design is meeting its objectives.

Although this is true, in our experience telling people that they can't use these phrases hampers the flow of a critique discussion. These two phrases are such a natural part of how many of us speak that it is inevitable that people will use them. If they've been informed that they can't use them and do inadvertently, they apologize, become flustered, and try to regroup, sometimes losing clarity around the point they were trying to make and causing some awkwardness in the exchange.

When someone states that he likes or doesn't like something in a critique, what's important is to then facilitate the conversation to understand whether his reasons are pertinent to the objectives of the design.

Central Idea

Having rules for critique helps to set expectations for others as to how the critique session should work. It also helps participants by providing guidelines and boundaries to the framework for sharing their insights and having productive conversations. The rules should be shared with others *before* the session; in fact, it's a good idea to post them in the meeting room.

Preparing for and Kicking Off a Critique

Getting a critique off on the right foot is important. Faulty starts can derail the discussion, causing confusion and a need to spend all our time getting everyone on the same page. Presenting quickly, reviewing the rules of critique, and focusing participants on specific aspects of the design are a few critical components of a good start.

WHO SHOULD WE INCLUDE?

Who participates in a critique is important and can affect the outcome of the session. We should look beyond just the design team for potential attendees. Consider other members of the project team as well, for example developers, marketing professionals, business analysts, product managers, subject matter experts (SMEs), project managers, and even executive stakeholders.

Even though there will be times when we'll want a smaller, more focused session with just the design team or people from a specific role, it's important to remember that anyone, regardless of role, can critique. By including a diverse group people from our team, we will open up the possibility for alternate viewpoints and ways of thinking analytically. Additionally, by including a range of disciplines as our attendees, we help build collaboration across the project team.

Additional consideration for who we'll include should be based on expertise related to the aspects of the design on which we wish to focus the critique. For example, if we are building a customer service application, it will be beneficial to invite someone from the customer support team to provide her insights, because she is close to the customer, and more than likely will be using the tool we are creating. SMEs do not need to have design background or knowledge; most of the time they will understand the need we're designing for, which makes their input very valuable.

As for the number of people to include, remember that critique is a conversation. Think about the maximum number of attendees who can carry on a single conversation without it splintering off into side discussions. In our experience, that's about six people. That doesn't mean that if we're in a position where we're required to have more people in attendance that we can't critique. It's just likely to take a bit more active facilitation, or perhaps the session will need to be broken into smaller groups.

ENSURE THAT THE TEAM KNOWS THE CRITIQUE SESSION FORMAT AND THE PLANS FOR FACILITATING IT

The people we invite to the session—whether they are designers or from another discipline—will have varying backgrounds and experiences with feedback and critique. Some might not be familiar with critique at all. Thus, it is important to set some expectations.

Particularly in formal critiques, but sometimes in informal ones as well, it is a good idea to begin by talking with participants about the type of discussion we're looking to have and any details about how we plan to facilitate the conversation. The less familiar a group is with critique, the more important this can become. We need to set expectations with regard to the kind of feedback we're interested in and why. Sharing the parts of the design you plan to focus on as well as critique rules is useful as well. The more the team understands about how the session is expected to go, the more they can come prepared to participate in a productive manner.

AVOID "TA-DA" MOMENTS

As designers, it is common for us to take the information we gather during research and analysis to our desks and work like a mad scientist on our creations. When the time is right we emerge with grand plans to show our awesome design to the team. We unveil our creation: "Ta-da! Look what I've made." And then we wait for the applause...

Crickets

The response we get is often not what we'd hoped for. Most, if not all of the people we're revealing our designs to are just seeing the designs for the first time and can only really have a gut reaction to what they are seeing. This is *reactive feedback*, and as we've described, it is rarely useful when it comes to helping us iterate and improve on our designs.

Critical thought takes a little bit of time. People need to think through a process or elements of a design, determine the effects they believe they'll have, and then compare those effects to the desired objectives. When we wait until the critique to show our work and expect immediate feedback, we put our team in a position to give us responses that they have not had the time to think through.

If possible, we suggest getting the designs that are going to be critiqued out to those participating in the meeting before the critique takes place. This gives participants the time to review the designs and think through their feedback and questions. Sending the designs out a couple of days in advance is often enough.

Now, we know what some of you are thinking: "No way! If I send out the designs ahead of time I will get a ton of feedback via email. People will be focusing on the wrong things, or I will just get a list of changes from people."

This is completely understandable. Or, perhaps no one will bother to look at what we've sent and so sending things out ahead of time feels wasteful. The truth of the matter is that no matter which route we choose, there will always be people who do their own thing. Still, we need to do what we can to avoid creating situations where reactions are all we can collect. By avoiding the "Ta-da!" moment approach we help our teams and clients to provide us with the feedback and insights that are needed to improve our designs.

To minimize participants getting stuck on an aspect of the design that might be irrelevant to that on which you plan to focus your critique discussion, limit what you send to only the relevant aspects of the design you plan to discuss. If you want to focus on one particular flow, don't send wireframes or storyboards for the entire product. Also, preface the designs with a few clear notes on what the critique will focus on and what you expect from participants. Figure 5-3 shows an example of an email Adam recently used on one of his projects.

Note that we aren't asking participants to come to the meeting with their feedback ready. Rather, we want to get them to begin thinking about the design and any questions they might have. What we're trying to do is jump-start the critical thinking process prior to the beginning of the conversation itself.

Yes, there are some people who will respond to your email with feedback. To be transparent with you, Adam did in response to the email in Figure 5-3.

Adam Connor

Sent: Thursday, July 24, 2014 at 9:24 AM

To: Adam Connor

📎: ➥ quickPractice-wireframes.pdf (2.9 MB); ➥ miniBrief.pdf (102.9 KB)   (Preview All)

Hey everyone,

Tomorrow afternoon is our next critique. This time around we're going to focus on the screens and flow related to the "quick practice" scenario. I've attached the applicable screens with annotations so you can see how a user would move through them. Please review these prior to the session.

As a reminder this scenario describes students using the app to quickly test their knowledge in short time frames, such as while their on the train to class in the morning. The goals and principles applicable to this scenario are:

- Increase correct answers: Increase the percentage of correctly answered questions by 5% over the students last practice session.
- Adapt to the student's understanding: As the student demonstrates stronger understanding, move them on to questions that build upon that understanding.
- Encourage the student: motivate the student to keep trying new questions and continue their practice.
- Ensure understanding: work to make sure that the student actually understands the material and is not simply guessing and getting lucky.

I've also attached the project mini brief in case anyone needs it.

Adam Connor
Experience Designer, VP Organizational Design & Training
Mad*Pow

FIGURE 5-3

An example of a sample critique session notification email

What we do in situations like this is reply to any feedback we might receive letting the sender know that we've noted it and that we'll plan to address it in the critique session. When the time for the critique session comes, we revisit the feedback we received from that individual. We ask if the feedback is still relevant now that more about the design has been discussed. As a result, the individual(s) who provided feedback either understands why decisions were made and rescinds her feedback, or the feedback is discussed further to gain more understanding.

By acknowledging the individual's feedback and then addressing it in the critique, we are letting her know that we are not dismissing this feedback, but we're also working on facilitating productive conversations. Although situations like this might not be ideal, they do provide the opportunity to improve facilitation and communication skills.

For situations in which you don't have the opportunity to send things out ahead of time, or perhaps you did and no one bothered to look at what you sent, simply pace the conversation a bit slower initially. Give people a chance to think critically. To do this, focus on smaller, more discrete aspects of the design at first and collect critique on those. Ask specific questions about a design element with respect to a particular goal or principle. Your objective here is to not overwhelm participants by dumping a lot of information on them all at once.

DESCRIBE THE PRODUCT'S OBJECTIVES

Whether you're sending out emails in preparation for the critique session or standing in front of the room presenting your work to the group, be sure to remind the team of the goals, principles, scenarios, and personas that apply to the aspects of the designs being reviewed. This will help provide the correct context for the participants to analyze the designs.

You don't need to go into great detail about how the product will meet those objectives, but it is important to keep these goals in the forefront of the team's mind so that they can focus and frame their feedback accurately. If you're using a tool such as a mini brief (see Chapter 3 for more on this), this can be as simple as doing a quick read-through of the pertinent elements at the very beginning of the meeting.

PRESENT YOUR WORK QUICKLY AND EFFICIENTLY

When presenting work for feedback it is a common urge to overexplain things to ensure that those critiquing really understand the design, the choices that were made, and the reasons why they were made. But this approach can often slow things down and eat up the time in the meeting.

We need to present efficiently. This doesn't mean that we have to rush through the presentation, but rather keep an efficient, steady pace. We should walk the team through the specific aspect of the design that we want to discuss and not worry about explaining our rationale for every decision; just give enough of an explanation so that the team gets an understanding of how the design is intended to work. If at some point we feel as though we went too quickly, we can make mention of it and ask if there are any questions or anything that we can clear up.

From there, more details about the effectiveness of decisions with regard to the project's objective, or the thinking behind decisions can come out as participants ask questions.

It is natural to want to dive into all the details of our design so that everyone understands what we are trying to accomplish, but it's more effective to let additional details, such as the rationale behind our decisions, come about as participants ask questions.

Allowing for questions to be asked is a critical part of an effective presentation. When we try to explain every detail up front, it's as if we're trying to avoid the potential for questions. We bombard participants with so much that they can become overwhelmed.

Another consideration for presenting efficiently is to focus your presentation on what isn't obvious or can't be seen easily (see Figure 5-4). Focus on talking about the aspects of the design that the participants can't see. Participants likely don't need to be made aware of the fact that the navigation is at the top of a web page followed by the header. A way we commonly do this is to present the design from the perspective of a user.

If we give a focused walkthrough and then prompt for questions—sometimes by starting to ask questions ourselves—we give participants the opportunity to tell us when they're ready for, or need, additional information to aid in their understanding and analysis. They get what they need when they need it. By allowing the details to come forward through the questions and conversation that happens during the critique, the details about the design and decisions we made are more closely tied to participant's insights and questions.

BE CAREFUL WHEN TALKING ABOUT CONSTRAINTS

While designing, teams will run into no shortage of constraints. These might stem from the workings of legacy systems, infrastructure limitations, deadlines, budgets, or a variety of other business or technical decisions. While initially presenting part of a design, it's not uncommon to want to include mention of the constraints we faced, especially if the constraint was particularly frustrating and forced us to make a decision that we feel is less than ideal. In these situations, however, some participants will often interpret the constraints we discuss as excuses or possibly even that we're casting blame. As a result, they can have a negative impact on the tone and energy of the discussion.

FIGURE 5-4
Example of improved presentation by focusing on describing the interactions and experience of a user

In these situations it's often better to let discussion of the constraint arise through questions. Wait for someone to ask about why choices were made and, if relevant, explain the constraint(s), choosing your words thoughtfully so that it doesn't sound as though you're blaming the constraint for a decision you wish was otherwise. Be as matter-of-fact about it as possible, and, if needed, set up additional time later to further discuss the constraint and its impact.

In some cases, it can also be useful to wait to discuss constraints after the critique is over and insights are being reviewed. Follow up with the person who provided the insight, discuss the constraint with them, and, if needed, bring in someone who can provide more information about the constraint and how you might be able to work around it.

There is one instance for which including a constraint in your presentation is appropriate: if you've discussed the constraint in a previous discussion with the group and are presenting your solution to it. In this case, the team is already aware of the constraint, and so how you addressed it is part of the context they need to help understand your presentation. Again though, be careful with wording and be as matter-of-fact as possible.

Central Idea

Proper preparation for a critique session can make a world of difference when it comes to getting the insights that will help improve what you are working on. Ensure that participants know what is being critiqued, how the sessions will be run, and what the goals of the session are.

The Facade of Authority

It's easy to assume that when you take on the role of a facilitator during any form of collaborative session, you earn a certain level of authority over the participants in the room. Sadly, this isn't the case. In fact, the authority you hold as a facilitator is only as strong as your personality and overall social presence.

Brad Nunnally, UX Solution Architect, Perficient

The true owners of the room are the participants of the session. If you happen to be dealing with a group of strong personalities or folks who are used to being the voice of authority in a room, your ability to effectively facilitate the group is going to be a fun little challenge.

I ran into this issue—my false authority as a facilitator was called out and it resulted in losing any resemblance of control or flow—during a series of collaborative workshops I was running.

The workshop that suffered the most was the design studio, which was supposed to result in a strong vision for the future that the client needed to help sell the need for a new platform and design for one of their internal applications. The worst part about it was that I was to blame.

As the group was beginning to settle in and I was about to review the purpose of a design studio and what would be expected of the participants, I asked if everyone would put away their laptops. No sooner had I asked for this small favor, than one of the more outspoken personalities responded with "Good luck with that!" After the laughter died down, I responded with a wisecrack of my own explaining how he had just shattered any sense of authority I had over the other participants. The result of this little joke was that all the participants became aware how little authority I really had, and they all refused to put away their laptops.

One of the biggest benefits of a design studio is the idea sharing and the various rounds of critique that occurs between the design iterations. Now, with their attention split between the activity and their laptops, the rounds of critique that followed were shallow. By the end of the session, there was little to no group consensus on the direction of the new solution or what kind of priority needed to be assigned to the various features.

I learned a very important lesson that day not only about how to facilitate a design studio and critique, but about facilitation as a whole. The trick is in becoming a group leader rather than an authority figure that is directing people to do things that might be outside of their comfort zone.

Several tools are necessary to make this happen, however:

An outline and agenda

> The most important tools, these set the tone of an activity and establish a defined set of rules for the session. These are documents that can be shared prior, and become something that helps to establish a social contract between you, the facilitator, and the group of participants.

A timetable

> This written-out breakdown of activities, discussion points, and breaks can be part of your written agenda or a standalone document. The timetable is something that is reviewed with the group at the start of a session, and it allows time to be the authority in the room, which you the facilitator are simply enforcing.

The more external artifacts that you can use as sources of authority, the easier it is for you to manage the flow of the conversation and maintain control over personalities that would normally overpower other participants and create an unproductive environment for collaboration, sharing, and critique.

Tools and Techniques for Effective Facilitation

It's important to have a tool set and planned strategies for dealing with various situations that might arise during a critique.

DEFINING THE CRITIQUE SCOPE AND GOALS

We need to determine scope and goals for the products we are creating in order to help us to stay on track and focus on our outcomes during the course of the project. Similarly, a successful critique should also have defined goals and scope to guide the team focused on collecting the relevant and desired insights of each session.

The scope of a critique is an identification of the components of the design that the team will be analyzing and the objectives against which they'll be analyzed.

For example, one session might focus on critiquing the visual styles of a design against a particular set of design principles, whereas another session might be focused on critiquing a specific sequence of screens and interactions against the relevant scenario and goals.

Setting the discussion parameters helps participants to know what to expect and to stay on track during the conversation and gives you a direction to steer back to when people begin discussions that are beyond the scope of the session.

For situations in which participants do begin to veer beyond the set parameters, we can now make note and plan for additional discussions while still getting the session at hand back on track to collect the insights we need at that point in time.

With the scope of a critique session set, identifying the goals can be fairly straightforward:

1. Identifying what is working in the designs with respect to the identified scope

2. Identifying anything that isn't working in the designs with respect to the identified scope

3. Gathering insights on any specific questions the designer may have

4. Identifying any concerns, open questions, and assumptions

Another way to identify goals and scope is to do *reverse planning*. In this approach, we begin by identifying what actions you want to be able to take after the conversation. From that identification, we can think about what questions we need answered in the critique in order to take those actions. And finally, understanding the questions we need to discuss and answer gives us an indication of the aspects of the design we need to present and focus our discussion on.

For example, imagine we're designing a new application for filing an auto insurance claim. Part of the design includes a new change in the filing process in which the customer can digitally submit photos of damage to get an appraisal in minutes. Imagine that we also know that a usability study is planned in the next few weeks that will focus on observing how people react and are able to use this new process.

This would imply that, going into our usability study, we want to ensure that our prototype is the best reflection of what the process and the experience using it would be.

So, given that we have some time to iterate between now and the usability study, then a logical scope would be to focus on the scenarios that would utilize this new claims process. Potential goals for this critique might be:

- Identifying the aspects of the design that do not support the desired experience.

- Identifying the aspects of the design that are most effective in producing the desired experience so that they can perhaps be expanded upon.

- Identifying the aspects of the design where there are the most questions or disagreement amongst the team, so that the usability study can take them into consideration and perhaps incorporate them into the study's plan

IMPLEMENTING ACTIVE LISTENING

Hearing is easy; listening is difficult. It sounds cliché, but it's true. We all interpret things in different ways. We all have a multitude of things going through our minds at any one time. And, we all have brains that are often more focused on getting our own perspective out than listening to and understanding that of someone else.

With a diverse group of participants (or even a group of only designers) this challenge becomes compounded. Vocabulary and understanding of terminology is going to vary among participants. We can't take everything communicated to us in a critique at face value and assume that everyone has the same understanding of what a piece of feedback means. We need to ensure that the designer as well as the rest of the team have a shared understanding of the insights being raised.

Active listening is when we reply to the feedback we're given by repeating it back as we've understood it. The person who originally gave the feedback can then confirm whether our understanding matches the point he was trying to communicate. Here is an example:

Product Owner: I have a concern about the placement of the news feed on the screen; it is very prominent, but I don't think our customers actually use it that much.

Designer: OK. If I understand you correctly you are concerned that this news feed, because it might not be used much, is attracting too much attention and can be distracting users from other more important elements? Am I correct in my understanding?

Product Owner: Yes, we should explore a different treatment so that we can give higher priority to something the customer uses more.

By responding to feedback in this manner we are able to validate whether our understanding is accurate.

After we have established that we have an understanding, we can discuss more details about the point being raised. For example, after the preceding exchange, the designer could ask about what in the current treatment of the newsfeed gives it significant prominence. Is it the placement, the type size, or some other aspect?

For those times when our understanding is inaccurate, we can then ask questions that dig into the feedback for further clarity. For example, in the previous exchange, if the product owner responded that the designer's understanding was inaccurate, the designer might respond with something like:

Can you help me understand a bit more about your concern about the news feed's prominence?

or:

OK. Let's look at this a little more. What might happen if we left it as prominent as it is?

By asking questions we can get more information to help us refine and adjust our understanding of the concern being raised. A particularly effective technique we've seen is illustrated in the second question. These kinds of questions prompt the participant to further describe the effect on the user, or the behaviors or actions that are undesirable, which we can then relate to the objectives of the product.

ADDING SIMPLE STRUCTURES: ROUND ROBIN AND QUOTAS

Sometimes, a group—particularly one that's new to critique—has trouble getting a conversation started. The group has difficulty letting the critique flow as naturally as a casual conversation would. People sit around looking at one another awkwardly, not sure what to do. In these cases, sometimes adding a very simple structure can give people a predicable format that lets them know what's expected.

One example of these simple structures is the *Round Robin*. When using Round Robin, the person facilitating the critique goes around the room in a specific, repeatable order, calling on and collecting feedback from participants. This eliminates waiting to see who speaks first. It also reinforces that everyone should participate and gives participants some predictability as to when they'll get the chance to share their feedback.

Round Robin doesn't need to be used for the entire duration of the discussion. In fact, we recommend you do not use it for the entire session. It can be a great way to get things started, but after the conversation is going, Round Robin doesn't exactly fit a natural flow, and forcing it unnaturally can hinder the critique.

We've also seen it used at the very end of a critique as a way to give everyone a chance to share anything they might not have gotten to during the critique.

Another structure to consider using is *Quotas*. With Quotas, the facilitator lets the team know that an objective of the critique is to collect a certain number of things that are working well and things that aren't (often two that aren't and one that is) from each participant. For example, each participant should share two aspects of the design that they feel are strong, and one that isn't. The formula of the quota can vary, and we definitely suggest trying different combinations of quotas to see what works most effectively.

With these types of structures, however, it's important to recognize that some groups can find them annoying because they seem too basic or, as we've heard on some occasions, "too grade-school."

So, think about your group before electing to use either of these techniques. Are there attitudes or past interactions that indicate your participants might have these kinds of interactions? Often we recommend waiting until a team clearly has difficulty getting a critique session started before bringing these structures up as a possible solution. With Round Robin, the facilitator doesn't even need to mention that she will be using the format to the attendees; she can keep that to herself as a structure for facilitating the critique.

When the conversation gets going, the facilitator can ease off of these structures and just let the critique happen naturally.

USING DIRECT INQUIRY

Sometimes, there might be a participant in a critique whose expertise is particularly relevant to the aspects of the design you're critiquing or the objectives for which you're designing. It's not uncommon for individuals in an organization to become the sole knowledge keeper for a particular business process or system. In these cases, it's perfectly acceptable to ask that individual directly for his thoughts.

> Years ago, I was on a project to redesign a customer service platform for a large organization. The company had a particular audience subset that had very specific needs and distinct processes from the others for a variety of complicated legal and compliance reasons. Because this audience was smaller, the service team that handled their issues was also small, and one individual who handled all of their training was considered to be the company expert.
>
> Although it was important that the design take into account all audiences and that I collect feedback from perspectives across the team, it was clear that there was still a knowledge gap. Even with the personas and scenarios taken from our research, no one on the team understood this small group of service reps and client the way our company expert did. And because this group was small, it was easy for conversations to leave them out.
>
> That meant that I, as a facilitator, needed to pay extra attention to ensuring that that didn't happen. In addition to focusing critique discussions on the relevant scenarios and personas, I would also pose questions directly to our expert, giving him a chance to share his perspective. This helped us to balance our conversations and precluded our missing key considerations for the design.
>
> **—ADAM**

By asking questions of people directly, we can be certain that we take advantage of the opportunities we have to gather perspectives that are particularly relevant to the information we want to capture in a critique. This also means that it's a good idea for the individual facilitating a critique to have an understanding of a participant's particular expertise so that he can be aware when a relevant question comes up and ensure that those individuals get a chance to share their thoughts.

PUTTING ON THE THINKING HATS (LENS-BASED ANALYSIS)

Similar to setting the scope of the critique, using *Thinking Hats* helps participants to frame their feedback in a certain context, making it a bit easier to maintain productive discussion and provide actionable feedback.

The Six Thinking Hats is a facilitation technique created by Edward de Bono, M.D., and described in the book he authored of the same name. The six hats method uses colored hats to represent different ways of analyzing a problem space or design. Throughout the session the team will switch hats to change perspective. Following is a description of each hat:

White hat

> The white hat takes the focus and puts it on facts alone for analysis, with no speculation.

Yellow hat

> The yellow hat represents looking at the positive, focusing on what is working.

Black hat

> The black hat focuses on concerns, difficulties, or why something might not work. Black-hat thinking is often seen when someone plays the role of devil's advocate.

Red hat

> The red hat focuses on feelings that participants have in response to what they are analyzing. Hunches, fears, emotional responses, and personal likes and dislikes all make up red-hat thinking.

Green hat

The green hat focuses on creativity and generating new concepts and understandings.

Blue hat

The blue hat identifies the individual who is managing the discussion, determining its focus, goals, and so on. It is the one hat that is not shared by the group.

The Six Thinking Hats is a lens-based analysis technique. When using the Six Thinking Hats, team members all wear the same color hat at the same time; this keeps everyone analyzing the designs through the same "lens," keeping the conversation focused.

While de Bono's version established six specific hats, teams can also come up with their own lenses to fit their context. For example, if working with multiple personas, teams might use each persona as a lens, analyzing the design for a particular scenario in the context of one persona's needs, expectations, and behaviors before moving on to another.

TAKING NOTES

Taking notes is a must for any formal critique, and it isn't a bad idea for informal ones, either. It's not uncommon for discussions to go so deep or so broad that people forget everything that was said. And when that forgotten feedback is something that could be valuable to iterating on a design, our efforts to facilitate great critiques lose some of their value.

Notes are the simplest way to ensure that everything is captured. They provide documentation of the points and ideas raised during the discussion, and the designer and team can review them later as needed.

We recommend that in a critique, one individual be designated as the note taker and that she records notes publicly. It's not unusual for people to take their own notes in meetings and then share them later, but our experiences have shown that this approach can be problematic. Each person's notes are their own interpretation of what is being discussed. Trying to merge notes from a group of people can be confusing and time consuming.

By having one individual take notes publicly—in a manner where everyone in the discussion can see what is being captured—we can avoid these challenges. This way the team members can look at exactly what is being written and question or clarify it if it does not match their understanding. There are a number of ways we can do this. It can be as simple as writing on an easel pad, or if presenting digitally, adding annotations or comments to screenshots in a tool such as Acrobat or InVision.

It's also useful to take note of how people participate. These notes aren't taken publicly as those just mentioned—that would be pretty awkward—but they are important. By watching how people participate during the session, we can see what facilitation techniques worked, and what didn't. We can see who is interested and participates and who is not interested. Then, we can use this information to determine how best to gather feedback from the team and who to invite to future critiques.

USING THIRD-PARTY FACILITATORS

Using a third-party facilitator—someone from outside the team or project—to run a critique can be helpful when a team is just beginning to implement regular critiques as a part of the design process. A third-party facilitator does not provide feedback on the design as a participant would. His role is purely to guide the conversation and keep it within scope by making sure people are able to ask questions and share their perspectives, while ensuring that those perspectives are understood by all participants. Because they control the flow of the conversation, the designer is better able to capture notes, present designs, clarify points, and respond to questions.

However, this shift in control can sometimes create challenges, too. The designer on the project will be responsible for acting on the insights collected, and is therefore best at understanding where clarification and further discussion is needed or where and how focus may need to shift during the conversation to be most effective. A facilitator, particularly one not familiar with the design decisions made or the everyday workings of the project, might not be able to pick up on when something that is useful has been shared, or how to guide reactive or directive feedback to a place of being useful.

This can create a lot of back and forth between the designer and the facilitator during the session. As a team becomes more comfortable with the critique process, it's advisable that they take on the facilitation responsibilities themselves.

HAVING THE DESIGNER PRESENT

It's not uncommon to encounter situations in which feedback is being collected and delivered when the designer isn't present. This often happens if the designs have been emailed around or a team member solicits feedback from other team members without the designer being involved. You've probably encountered this: designs are presented, maybe in a meeting or in an email, and the team is asked to follow up in a few days with their feedback. When that feedback begins coming in, there is some trouble deciphering it, and lengthy, difficult-to-follow email chains begin passing around the group. Sometimes, these can go on for days. Or, maybe a new meeting is scheduled to review all of the feedback, basically making all of the back and forth emails a waste anyway.

Whenever possible, critiques should include the designer and should be done via real-time conversation. If the designer is not present, other team members are forced to make assumptions about why the designer chose a certain line of thinking and made certain decisions. And using tools such as email inhibits a team's ability for clear dialogue.

> "If the designer were here I could ask her questions, but she isn't, so I just have to guess at what she was trying to accomplish."

> "I think my critique is right but I have no way to know, because the designer isn't here to tell me what her goals were or the problems she's trying to solve."

When critique sessions are held and the designer isn't present, it puts both the person giving critique and the person receiving critique at a disadvantage. All the insights shared are based on assumptions, which is a shaky foundation upon which to base our iterations and improvement.

Nevertheless, it's important to recognize that there will be situations in which having the designer present won't be possible. When providing feedback under these circumstances it is best to note in your feedback the assumption that is being made so that the designer can first identify whether it matches with her actual objectives. This means that there might be some wasted feedback, but that is one of the trade-offs when conducting critiques in this manner.

Central Idea

To keep a critique on track and effective, we need to be able to react and respond to situations as they arise. Familiarize yourself with a variety of techniques and the situation they best fit so that you're prepared to handle whatever comes up.

Collecting Critique and Doing Something with It

Getting people talking about a design is great, but it doesn't mean much if what's discussed isn't used to improve the design. After the discussion is finished, we need to have a plan for what we'll do with what has been collected.

Following up a critique is crucial to keeping things moving forward. Critique is an active, living dialogue that lasts the lifespan of a product. Here are some tips on how to follow up in a way that keeps the conversation moving in a productive manner:

SHARE THE NOTES AND THE DESIGN THAT WAS ANALYZED (IF YOU HADN'T ALREADY)

Remember that notes should be taken publicly so that everyone can see what's being captured during the critique. It would be odd for the designer to take those away and keep them for himself.

Those notes can be of use to the entire team as they work on their respective parts of the project. They're also useful in future conversations as a way to refer back and refresh people's memories about what was discussed.

DOCUMENT ANY OPEN QUESTIONS AND
PLANS TO GET THEM ANSWERED

Using the notes from the session, pull out and create a separate list of any open questions or assumptions that need to be looked into further.

For example, if you're working on an application for handling insurance claims, you might find that during critique you identify an assumption such as, "We're assuming that business rules require that we have all of the requested information from a customer before a claim is filed and begins to be processed."

Calling out assumptions like this is important. You might not have someone in the conversation who can immediately verify whether the assumption is true. Sometimes, an unknown like this will be so significant that it's best to wait and get clarification before making a decision on changes related to it.

However, that's not where things end. After the critique, it's important that the team follows up on these assumptions and questions. Take the time to list them, share them with the team, and, if applicable, assign any responsibilities to team members for following up on specific items.

This is something that you can share via email or in something like Basecamp, where everyone involved can refer to them. This is helpful for keeping communication going and verifying that nothing slips through the cracks.

REVIEW THE FINDINGS

As the designer or part of the design team, the next step is to look over what was discussed to determine how it will be used or acted upon. People will have their own approaches to exactly how they do this, but here is Adam's:

1. Go through and fix any minor "quick hits," that is, typos, copy-paste errors, and small alignment issues.

2. Create a to-do list by reorganizing the notes and framing insights as actions. For example, a note such as, "The news feed is too prominent, because..." would be changed to, "Explore options for decreasing the prominence of the newsfeed...."

3. Go through the to-do list and try to organize it in some sort of loose priority. To be quite honest, there is no formula for this; it changes a little with every project depending on the team, culture, timeline, and so on. Here are the kinds of things I consider:

  ○ **Relevancy of the feedback to the product's objectives.** The more of the product's scenarios, personas, goals, and principles that the feedback is applicable to, the higher its priority.

  ○ **Immediacy of the feedback.** Based on the timeline and project plan, if there are certain aspects of the product that need to be addressed sooner than others, perhaps because they're planned to be developed or released sooner, those receive higher priority.

  ○ **Amount of agreement.** Thinking about the participants, I consider how many people shared the same perspective. Typically, the more people who agree on something, the higher priority that something receives.

  ○ **Source of the feedback.** I also consider who the feedback came from and that individual's knowledge and expertise. If it's particularly relevant to the feedback, perhaps because they're a subject matter expert, that can shift the priority.

  (As Adam says, this is completely unscientific.)

4. Go through and, using the priority, determine which items won't be addressed. Remember that just because something is said in a critique does not mean that something will change in the design as a result of it. For those items that won't be addressed, I note why, because I need to be ready to answer why it wasn't changed when it comes up in future discussions.

  I now have a to-do list that I can use with the team to iterate on the design.

FOLLOW UP WITH THE TEAM

After the critique is over, send an email to the participants thanking them for their involvement, laying out next steps, and specifying when the next session will be held and what will be covered in that session. If some of this information is still to be determined, it is OK to send updates when it is confirmed.

Also, let people know that you'll be following up with them to explore specific feedback and ideas further or to answer open questions. Set up times for additional conversations or collaborative activities.

These follow-ons are also effective in working through individual feedback that might be too vague or too complex. Whereas in a critique session there isn't time to unpack every detail of the feedback and explore solutions, following up with individuals provides the opportunity to dig deeper.

The key in all of this is to keep the momentum going.

Central Idea

Critique is a living process that continues through the life of a product. Follow up after sessions with next steps, insights gathered during the session, and outstanding questions to keep momentum moving forward and the process alive.

Wrapping Up

Facilitation is critical to the success of a critique. We must have a plan for what we want to discuss and understand as well as tools and structure that help us keep conversations moving in the right direction.

Some basic rules help us set up a critique and keep it focused and useful:

- Everyone is equal
- Everyone participates
- Avoid problem solving
- Don't rush to make decisions

Rules set the foundation, but how do we get ready for and start a critique discussion? If we aren't prepared and don't help our teammates and clients to be prepared, we are setting them up to provide us reactionary feedback. Making sure everyone understands what the focus of the critique is and has the materials needed is crucial:

- **Choose who is best to include.** Good insights can come from anywhere, not just the design team, so think about inviting a cross-functional group.

- **Let people know how the session will be run.** Let people know how you plan to run the session and collect their feedback.

- **Avoid "Ta-da!" moments.** Showing people a design and expecting them to be able to immediately give you useful, actionable feedback doesn't work.

- **Describe objectives.** People need to know what the design is trying to accomplish. Remind everyone so that participants are all on the same page.

- **Present quickly and efficiently.** Don't become bogged down explaining every detail of the design.

- **Be careful when talking about constraints.** Including them as part of your initial presentation can seem like you're making excuses. Let the issue of constraints come up through questions.

With the critique off and running, we need tools to help us facilitate the conversation as it develops:

- **Critique scope and goals.** Set the context and boundaries for the conversation. If the discussion begins to fall outside of your limits, by having these explicitly set, you can steer the conversation back within them.

- **Active listening.** Repeating back an insight or observation as you've understood it so that someone can confirm if your understanding matches the intent of that person.

- **Simple structures.** Formats such as Round Robin or Quotas can ease some apprehension and give people a predictable structure within which to work.

- **Direct inquiry.** Asking questions of people directly ensures that you take advantage of their expertise and experience with a topic.

- **Thinking hats/lenses.** Focus the conversation on a single aspect or angle at one time.

- **Notes.** Take notes publicly so that participants can verify that what is being captured matches what they're trying to say.

- **Facilitators.** Use a third party to manage the flow of the conversation. Although this can be helpful at first, as a team gains experience, it's better that it take on this role.

Nothing kills a great critique like poor follow-through. Be sure to use the insights you gather effectively and keep the momentum going.

- Share the notes and any open questions or assumptions that came up during the discussion.

- Review the findings and determine how to act on them.

- Follow up with people for further discussions or to explore ideas as you iterate.

There are a lot of tools and techniques in this chapter; some might work for you and some might not. The key is to get started, use the tools you think will work, critique how things went, make adjustments, and then try again.

[6]

Critiquing with Difficult People and Challenging Situations

We work in diverse settings; our teams are made up of people with different skillsets, backgrounds, experience levels, and approaches to building products. Diversity is an important aspect in creative collaboration. These differences between teammates means that we can draw inspiration from a wider array of possibilities; we have more material with which to build connections, increasing our chances of finding new, innovative solutions to the challenges we're trying to solve.

Yet, bringing people together in this way also means we need to be aware of and prepared for the challenges that are bound to arise. Take a group of individuals, put them together, and give them problems to solve, constraints, and deadlines, and it becomes inevitable that we will run into situations in which communication becomes a bit rough. Team members will disagree or people will misunderstand one another while discussing their ideas and designs, sometimes making things uncomfortable and slowing down the task to which you've been assigned.

This is perfectly normal. In no way does the presence of these challenges mean that we should cease collaborating. The fact of the matter is that regardless of how much effort we put into setting up conversations and critiques the right way, there will be situations for which things simply don't go according to plan. Occasionally, there will be people who don't participate in a productive manner for any number of reasons.

When these situations arise, the key is to identify where or when it is happening, identify the source, and work to understand what the individual(s) is trying to communicate.

Chapter 5 looks at some key techniques and best practices for facilitating these discussions, whether they are with our teams or with clients, and discusses focusing feedback on critique in order to produce analysis that's useful to moving a design forward. But the question still looms, "What do I do when others don't follow these suggestions or best practices?"

We might ask for critique and instead receive a list of requested changes. Or, we might get back a description or drawing of the solution that someone else thinks we should have come up with. We might get comments like, "This is horrible" or "Great work!" that leave us with very little understanding as to whether our designs might actually meet our objectives. And, we can expect that at some point in our careers as sure as the sky is blue we will encounter someone with whom it is just plain difficult to converse.

It should be noted that not every person providing less-than-useful feedback is doing so with underhanded, world-domination driven motives. Some individuals are trying to be helpful but are going about it the wrong way. For most situations, we've found that although our initial reaction to these situations might be negative or defensive, it's important to recognize that the feedback we receive from others might be founded in something that's worthwhile to understand. Even though we can't stop unclear or negative criticisms, we can change our perspective and try to find something of value in them.

Central Idea

There are going to be times when conversations and situations become challenging for a variety of reasons. Be prepared for them and don't lose heart. Understanding the situation you're in is the first step to forming a plan to work through these challenges.

Dealing with Difficult People

Certainly, we'd all prefer not to work with "difficult people," but they can't always be avoided. Some might be difficult because they're quiet and difficult to extract information from. Some can be difficult because it's not easy for them to communicate the points they're trying to get across. Others might be difficult because they have attitudes, intentions, or motivations that don't align with the principles of good critique or collaboration.

Whatever the reason, having tactics for working with and getting useful feedback from people like this is important.

SETTING THE RIGHT EXPECTATIONS

Sometimes, difficulties arise when people have different expectations about what they're being asked to do or how to do it. Addressing this is pretty straightforward. As is discussed in Chapter 5, making sure participants are aware of the format of the critique and how you plan to facilitate it is important in and of itself. It becomes even more important for situations in which we think some participants might present challenges.

It might seem a bit like overkill, but prefacing critiques like this can be truly helpful when participants or exchanges become challenging. Specifying the rules, structure, and focus for the critique at the outset can act as a preventative measure by encouraging people to pay more attention to how they participate and contribute to the critique.

Additionally, by communicating the rules of critique and specifying what we plan to focus our conversation on (see Chapter 5) ahead of time or at the beginning of the meeting, we have something to refer back to if during the course of the critique someone begins straying outside the rules or focus. As a facilitator, this strengthens our ability to address challenges as they arise and, by extension, keep critiques a safe, comfortable environment for our teams to discuss their designs and perspectives.

Along these lines, as we've mentioned before, posting the rules for critique in the meeting invite and the meeting room itself so that team members can become familiar with them and refer to them easily is very helpful, as is posting or documenting the specific goals and focus of the conversation.

AVOIDING PERSONAL PREFERENCES AND MOTIVATIONS

As discussed in Chapter 3, many project teams and organizations that have trouble collecting useful feedback suffer from not having a common foundation, a set of decisions that frame and form the objectives of the product.

Having an agreed upon and mutually understood set of goals, principles, personas, and scenarios not only provides for more useful and relevant critique, it also serves as a great tool for refocusing conversations on the product and away from criticism that is rooted in personal preference or misaligned motivations.

Depending on the details of the critique we receive, we can ask the individual to frame it in relation to a goal, scenario, principle, or persona. For example, consider the following dialogue:

> **Critic:** There are too many things to click on this screen! I think we should move some to other screens. It's too confusing.
>
> **Designer:** OK. Can you tell me a little more about your concern? Is there a particular persona or scenario that this is likely to be problematic for?
>
> **Critic:** Any of them. There's just too much... I dunno, maybe the service rep. If I was a service rep on a call with a customer I wouldn't be able to find what I need to click on with all of these options.
>
> **Designer:** Great. Let's think more about that. We know that when a call comes in, CSRs are trying to handle the customer's request as quickly as they can. And part of the issue in the current scenario is that the options they need are buried within too many different screens.
>
> **Critic:** Yes, but there's just so much going on here. I'm concerned they won't know where to click.
>
> **Designer:** OK, so it sounds like you want to make sure that the options are well organized so that CSRs can find them as quickly as possible. Is that accurate?

In this example, by pulling in the foundational elements of the CSR persona and information from a scenario involving their use of the screen being discussed, we're able to take what might start off seeming like personal opinion and bring it to a concern that we can further discuss in the critique and, if relevant, work to address in the next iteration.

This also highlights the importance of knowing about our product's users and their needs, behaviors, and so on. Having solid, relevant research that we can reference is a great way to make sure your critiques stay grounded.

Central Idea

Addressing difficulties that come up during the course of a conversation entails being able to identify issues and having tools to address them. Setting up conversations with shared references such as rules, objectives, focus, and so on provides a foundation for us to use throughout the critique.

PREVENTING SURPRISES FROM QUIET PARTICIPANTS

Why can quiet people be difficult? Because sometimes they're a ticking time bomb.

OK, maybe that's a bit alarmist, but we've seen quiet people be problematic on more than one occasion. Sometimes, these individuals have something valuable to share, but for any number of reasons they don't share it during the session or even with you at all. There are times when this silence is a result of someone feeling overwhelmed by the process and subject matter. Other times it mght be because they are afraid to provide information that might be considered "wrong."

Instead, they share it with someone else, perhaps another teammate or a manager, and then the comment travels person to person until finally making its way back to you, days or even weeks later when you might no longer be able to act upon it.

When collecting feedback in a meeting, look for people who are not saying much. Take steps to ensure that they have opportunities to share their thoughts by asking them for feedback, directly if necessary, and try to make them feel more comfortable. It can be useful to frame the feedback request as something relevant to their specific expertise or skillset.

Be cautious, though: you don't want to overwhelm people by continuously putting pressure on them to contribute. If you get the sense that an individual just hasn't found something useful to say, leave it at that. It could be that they're just quiet or shy, and your best approach could be to try to talk with the person one on one after the session.

USING LADDERING TO EXPAND ON FEEDBACK

Ever hung out with a child around the age of 3 to 6? If so, then you know what it's like to be asked the question "Why?" over and over again. Children often do this when trying to get adults to explain challenging concepts to them.

The repeated asking of the question "Why?" can be used to help an individual to gradually get more specific or provide more details about a subject. *Laddering*, a technique commonly used in design research, uses the repeated asking of "Why?" in various forms to understand the cause or rationale behind a statement made by an interview participant. Specifically, with each answer the individual provides, we respond with a form of the question "Why?" as a way to get him to provide more information until we reach a logical stopping point. A similar method, called the "5 Whys," is often used in projects to determine the root cause of a problem to be solved.

This same basic technique can be applied in design discussions when we want to understand more about the feedback someone is giving and why they're giving it. This is especially helpful when someone provides feedback that we sense may be related to her personal preference. By asking her "Why?" progressively, we're likely to get one of two potential results:

- As we continue to ask questions about the feedback she has shared, we will uncover details about what she is trying to communicate in a way that ties back to the objectives of the product. Or...

- We may lead her to realize that her feedback is based more on her personal preference and motivations rather than the objectives of the product and therefore it should be left alone and the conversation can move on.

For example:

Stakeholder: I think we should use less blue in the design.

Designer: What is it about the design that is leading you to think that?

Stakeholder: It's too much. If I squint my eyes, blue is the dominant color.

Designer: Why is it important that blue not be the dominant color in the design?

Stakeholder: We're trying to stand out from our competitors, and almost all of their sites are some shade of blue.

The way you ask "Why?" is very important to the success of this technique. In some situations the simple question of "Why?" can be seen as interpreted as aggressive or accusatory, and that sense can become significantly stronger with repetition. So it's recommended that you work toward wording your why's in a way that is more akin to an invite for the individual to continue sharing.

ATTEMPTING DIFFERENT DYNAMICS: ONE-ON-ONE CONVERSATION

People's behaviors and attitudes in a conversation can change depending on the size of the group conversing as well as the people who make up the group. Sometimes, it's these factors that are the cause for someone to be difficult to work with in a feedback discussion.

People can become uncomfortable or intimidated by large groups or a subject matter (design) with which they are not very familiar, so they withdraw. Others might try to dominate a conversation. Some people will have strong or combative personalities and become disruptive during critiques. As you work with your teams and clients, observe how they communicate and interact with others and make note of any concerns so that you are aware of them before you get into a meeting or critique with them.

Adam and I have found that in cases for which you know or suspect someone might have these kinds of challenges—they might have difficulty speaking up in groups, or they can be intimidating to a fair number of team members, preventing them from speaking up—reaching out to these individuals in advance to analyze the work with them alone and collect their feedback can prevent tough situations during the group critique.

First, by talking with them prior to the meeting, we will have already discussed the designs, which for individuals who have a tendency to intimidate others can lead them to not be as vocal during the meeting. This is because they have already provided insights, which can preclude opportunities for them to be difficult or disruptive during a session. Alternatively, if they do become challenging in the critique, we can refer back to the feedback and any agreements from your prior conversation with them and keep them accountable to those commitments.

We have also found that talking to these types of participants in advance can often make them feel that they have received your attention and have been heard. As a result, they sometimes feel that they can then forego attending the group critique, which can be helpful if their presence might have hindered other participants from giving useful feedback.

Central Idea

To deal with issues that can come up in a critique, you need to know what kinds of questions to ask as well as knowing when to ask them, even if that means doing it as part of a separate discussion.

Coping with Challenging Situations

Difficult people can show up at any time in any environment. We've already talked about some strategies for working with them, but hopefully, as you read the previous sections and thought about your own experiences, you've realized that in many cases, it isn't the person themselves that is inherently difficult, it's the situation or the way in which certain individuals deliver their feedback.

Here are some common situations that we've observed in the organizations we've worked with and some techniques for working through them.

CRITIQUING THE WORK OF SOMEONE AVERSE TO CRITICISM

Sometimes, the difficult situation lies not in receiving feedback, but giving it. As we know and have discussed, receiving feedback can be hard to do without taking it personally. Some people will take it better than others.

If we know that the individual whose work we need to analyze has trouble with receiving critique because they tend to get defensive or feel defeated, how do we go about making it easier for her? We don't want to hold back our comments. We need to be truthful. But we also need to show tact to keep the momentum and collaborative spirit of the team going.

Chapter 2 shares advice for giving critique, but here are some more thoughts when the person you're giving that critique to is particularly sensitive to feedback.

Get them talking

Engage them. Get them talking about the design, about the objectives of the product and the elements or aspects of the design that are intended to achieve those objectives. For some people, receiving feedback can cause them to freeze up or go silent. Get them talking and thinking critically about the work with you. Ask questions. Keep it casual and conversational.

As they talk more, most people tend to relax. As you ask questions and they work to describe the design and provide more details, they'll likely begin to analyze the design and participate in the critique not just as a recipient, but as a critic as well, which tends to make them more receptive.

Talk about the work, not the person

With people who are particularly sensitive to feedback, it's even more important to ensure that the conversation you have and the language you use center on the design and not the designer (see Figure 6-1).

Instead of...

Try something more like...

FIGURE 6-1

A demonstration of how to frame questions and critique on the design rather than the designer

This can be tricky. In critiques we want to make sure that the discussion includes the thoughts and reasoning people used when making design decisions. However, the more our questions seem to be about the designer, the more individuals who are sensitive to feedback can feel like the feedback is about them and not the design.

Emphasize that the critique is about iteration

When you're sensitive to feedback, it can be easy to forget that critique is about iteration and that the reason for critiquing work is because you plan to continue working on a design and use the insights taken from the critique to make it stronger.

Remind the recipient of this if you can during the feedback. Let him know that you're curious to see what he comes back with in the next iteration. If you've critiqued this work with him in the past, talk about how things have improved over the past iterations.

The sandwich method

The sandwich method is an often-talked-about method for delivering negative feedback in management circles. In it, you begin by presenting a piece of positive feedback, followed by the negative feedback you have, followed by another piece of positive feedback.

The idea is that by starting off positive you give the recipient a sense of success and support, so that when he receives the negative feedback you're about to follow up with, he doesn't feel as bad about it and his emotions don't fall as far. Then, another piece of positive feedback lifts his emotions again and, because there was more positive than negative, he feels like he's leaving with the scales tipped in a positive direction.

For as much anecdotal support as there is for the sandwich method, there is also a lot of criticism and skepticism as well as research that it doesn't work, mostly because of how it's often carried out. In many cases, the positive comments are superficial and or vague (Figure 6-2). They might be about a quality that has very little to do with what's being discussed, or about no strength at all really.

Most people can see right through these kinds of comments and they do little to help the situation. The initial praise or positive comment does little more than signal that something bad is coming. Additionally, because cognitively we expend more energy and attention processing negative situations than positive ones, initial positive comments are forgotten as soon as negative comments are brought in. And for some, the whole method can feel manipulative.

FIGURE 6-2
An example of a bad feedback sandwich

We strongly believe that balancing conversation around strengths and weaknesses of a design is important in a critique. And we agree that starting off on a positive note can be helpful in setting tone.

Most important though, is that the positive comments be about real strengths in the design (Figure 6-3); they should be aspects that we have thought about critically and feel are effective and important to the objectives of the project, not just things we came up with at the spur of the moment to make a weakness we want to point out easier to handle.

Don't worry about the "sandwich". Be honest with the recipient. Balance the conversation. Think critically about and discuss the elements of the design that work for and against objectives. And don't manipulate or make up insights and feedback just to try and make things easier.

FIGURE 6-3
An example of a balancing discussion of strengths and weaknesses

RECEIVING UNSOLICITED FEEDBACK

If feedback only ever happened when we ask for it, would it ever happen at all? The truth is feedback happens all the time whether we ask for it or not. Sometimes, it's conscious feedback, someone deliberately responding to something we've done by making comments or suggestions or asking questions. Sometimes it's subconscious. We might create or do something and notice a subtle change in someone's demeanor or behavior, or maybe a facial expression.

Feedback is a regularly occurring and natural part of our interactions with others. Whether we're solo creators or part of a team creating something, if we set a goal of wanting to improve our creations, we need to understand that feedback is constantly happening outside the situations in which we've requested it. It's up to us to recognize when feedback is occurring, work to understand what that feedback is telling us, and determine if it is useful in our work and whether we should pay attention to it.

Step 1: Be ready

Understanding that feedback occurs so frequently and naturally, it's best that we be proactive in thinking about how we want to handle it. Before sharing your work, even if you have no plans to ask for it, think about how you want to handle feedback. Spending a little time thinking about how you'll respond to compliments, questions, and critique can go a long way, not only toward making those exchanges much more useful to you as you iterate on your work, but also to helping you learn how to separate yourself from your work.

Separating yourself from your work can be difficult. You've put time and energy into what everyone else is now going to analyze with a critical eye. It's intimidating. One thing that has helped Adam and me to create this separation is remembering that critique is a tool that can help us produce better work. The focus of the critique is the product, not the person who created the work. If there is feedback that something missed the mark, it is OK, and the chances are pretty good that I am still an upstanding person. Critique is not about judgment, it is about refinement.

Step 2: Hold on to your reaction

When unsolicited feedback to something you've created or presented occurs—it might be verbal (someone saying or writing something) or physical (a physical gesture via body language or facial expression)—the first thing to do is to hold back your initial reaction. It's inevitable that we'll have a reaction, and the more passionate or pronounced the feedback is to which we're reacting, the stronger our reaction is likely to be.

What we need to do is give ourselves time to process the feedback and decide what we want to do with it. Do we want to learn more about why someone feels the way they do about the design? Would knowing it be useful to us in improving the design? Are we in a position where we could use that information?

Keep in mind that this applies for both positive and negative feedback. Even though feedback is positive, it might not be helpful. Someone saying, "I like this" might make us feel good, but the question remains, what does he like? People will often offer positive feedback because they don't want to hurt someone's feelings, not necessarily because they think the work is heading in the right direction. With all feedback, the best approach is to thank the individual for his feedback, be sure that you understand what he is communicating, review his feedback in light of what your known objectives are, and then follow up with questions.

Step 3: Consider the source and intent

What kind of feedback is it? Is it reaction, direction, or critique? Is it constructive or destructive? (We'll talk a bit more specifically about working with reactive and directive feedback in the next two sections.) If we can get a read on what type of feedback we're starting with, we can get a better sense of how to dig deeper to get something of value from it. The key question to ask though is "Why?" Asking "Why?" engages the critic and prompts her to explain and even rationalize her statements. Even feedback that might seem initially destructive can have some legitimate analysis behind it.

This doesn't mean that you should always engage with someone who is tearing your work apart. You should think about the source itself. If this is someone with a history of being a problem and you can ignore her comments, you probably should. But it might be someone who has something worthwhile to tell you and is just having some difficulty moving past that initial reactionary phase of feedback. Asking "Why?" often helps us see if this is the case.

You should also consider the view from which her feedback is coming. Is she speaking as a representative of the audience for whom you've created the design? Does she have expertise in a particular aspect touched upon by your creation? Or maybe she's just insightful? Again, the question "Why?" can help us determine the lens being used to derive the feedback we're receiving, making it possible for us to determine if we should pay attention to it in our next iteration or not.

Step 4: Listen, understand, and use it
If you've determined that the feedback might have something of use to it, you're next job is to listen. Pay attention. Be sure you really understand what you're being told. Use active listening and question for clarity by repeating back what you've heard but worded differently.

And finally, just as with any solicited critique, you can factor these new insights into your next iteration—assuming that you've determined they're applicable.

DEALING WITH REACTIVE FEEDBACK

> Well... it's better than peanut butter and salami!

No kidding, Adam actually witnessed that feedback in a meeting. After an awkward WTF moment in everyone's heads as they looked around the room at each other and wondered what a comment like that could possibly mean, the team learned that it definitely wasn't positive. It roughly translated to, "It's not the most heinous thing I've ever seen, but it's close."

This kind of feedback is bound to happen at some point in time. It might not be as extreme as a noxious combination of sandwich fillings. You might just get a "meh" or maybe something on the positive side like, "I love it!"

Remember that reactionary feedback comes from the more impulsive of our mental processes. It can be positive or negative, and it can come from one of a few different causes, as described in Chapter 1.

In general, though, this type of feedback is the result of an individual expressing a gut reaction to what they are seeing. They haven't taken the time to think critically, moving past that initial reaction to examine it and uncover the cause for it.

And, as we've described, this kind of feedback isn't very useful to us as we work toward iterating and improving our creation. It doesn't tell us what aspects of our creation will or will not work to achieve our objectives. Therefore, it doesn't help us identify which aspects of our creation should be changed, explored further, or expanded upon.

There is, of course, the possibility that the critic is just being difficult or their personality makes it challenging to work with them. In this case, it is natural to want to tell someone to kick rocks. Although this can bring some temporary gratification, it usually only complicates matters in the end. It's natural to grow defensive when criticism is coming our way; we must resist that urge and focus on the best solution.

As with unsolicited feedback, sometimes people aren't being trolls and might actually have valuable insights. Look to find the balance between not feeding the trolls and not becoming defensive, and collecting information that might be useful as you iterate on your design.

The only way to get someone to move past the reactionary phase of feedback is to ask questions that push him to examine not only his reaction, but also the creation you're asking them to analyze. Remember, at this point he's really only just reacted. His slower, more analytical cognitive processes that facilitate critical thinking haven't taken over yet. By asking questions, we can help ensure that they do. By asking questions, we can work toward exposing and understanding what it is that led the individual to give his reaction. As we converse and try to gather insights, we can then begin to determine if the individual is trying to be helpful and maybe just going about it the wrong way or if he is trolling or voicing an opinion with no real desire to help.

It's also important as you move through this process to pay attention to how you word your questions. It's important to try to word things in such a way that they aren't misconstrued as defensive and adversarial. Instead, you're looking to invite the individual to provide you with more of his thinking.

Step 1: Get more specific
The first question to ask is pretty straightforward:

> Can you tell me a bit more about what aspects of the design aren't working?

Of course you'll reword this depending on the specific reaction you've received. The key point is to try to get her to be more specific. Get her to focus on specific aspects or elements of the creation to which she is reacting. This way, you can better focus the rest of the conversation by discussing those aspects specifically, or perhaps the part of the design that you're interested in gathering feedback on is different from what she's reacting to, and so you can now try to steer her toward only paying attention to that part of the design.

Step 2: Talk about the "whys" and "hows"

Presuming that you're digging deeper into the critic's reaction (as opposed to discovering that she's reacting to something irrelevant to what we're trying to collect feedback on and refocusing the conversation) the next step is to understand the following:

- Why is/are the aspect(s) she is reacting to terrible?

- How does that relate to the objectives of the design itself?

This is where having a solid foundation really matters. If the team has already agreed upon things such as personas, goals, principles, and scenarios, you can ask people to relate their feedback to those foundational elements.

By uncovering this information, you can begin to get to the core of what the individual's problem with the design might be. Adam and I have found that, oftentimes, using this approach you, together with the critic, will be able uncover whether the feedback being given is pertinent or a matter of the critic's personal preference or motivations. By doing so, you help the critic understand the process of critical thinking so that in the future she's better able to give critique.

It isn't easy to discern what someone's motivations are. How she responds to the questions will help in understanding if she really is trying to help and just having a hard time communicating, or if she has other motivations.

One way to work through these difficulties is to reinforce and remind her that you are on the same team and working together. Use phrases such as, "I need your help to better understand" or "We really want to make sure this product meets its goals, and your help is crucial in accomplishing that." By doing this we can move away from a me-versus-you situation and put the focus on working together as a team to resolve differences and focus on the needs of the products.

Most, but not all, individuals will be cooperative in these situations and in those few cases of individuals who aren't, it is best to move on. If someone is nonresponsive to your attempts to reach out for clarification or he does not get any less difficult as the conversation progresses, this is probably a sign that you will not be able to make much progress with this person, and it will not be worth the time following up with him. In these cases, it is OK to thank the person for his insights and move on, focusing on collecting helpful insights on another topic or from others. Take note of how this person interacted so that you know what to expect from him in the future. In some cases, it might mean that you go about collecting his feedback in another way. In others, in which the individual is not a part of the project, it may mean that you exclude him from future critiques.

In the end, we should strive to see if we can get any information that can be used to improve the design by using some of the tips and techniques for facilitating critique we talk about in Chapter 5, even if we don't fully agree with an individual's overall assessment. Although it is not ideal when an individual's intent is not coming from a position of trying to be helpful, we can make the best of the situation by objectively analyzing the feedback he is providing, looking for anything useful.

Remember, this applies to positive feedback as well

When talking about feedback and criticism, it's easy to fixate on the negative. When we think about problems with getting feedback, that's where our minds instinctively go: to all the times when someone has berated us and told us our work is awful. Or, if it hasn't happened yet, we are consumed by the anticipation that it will one day, and what will we do then.

Nonetheless, we need to remember that reactionary feedback can be positive, too, even neutral. In these cases, even though our own reactions to the feedback we're receiving might not be so negative—it feels great when someone exclaims, "I love it" about something you've made—the feedback itself is still unhelpful in providing us with information to use in iterating on and improving our creation.

Thus, we still need to do our due diligence to ask questions and push people to think critically about our design and their reaction. What do they love about it? Why? How does it apply to our goals, personas, scenarios, and principles?

DEALING WITH DIRECTIVE FEEDBACK

Many of us have been in situations in which instead of getting what we'd consider to be useful feedback on our designs, we get a list of changes to make to it or suggestions on how we might improve it. Often, this list doesn't include a clear indication of why the changes should be made. Beyond that, some of the changes might be things that are detrimental to the design and things we'd advise against.

The most challenging, and possibly most frustrating, of these kinds of situations is when we don't receive actionable critique; instead, we get a sketch or mockup for a new design that the person we've asked for feedback has put together on her own.

We sit and stare at the screen with a million thoughts and questions running through our heads and often a building sense of frustration and insult.

How dare they!!! What do I do now?!?

Step 1: Calm down and let your reaction pass

Step back and force yourself to remember that most people are not diabolical, intentionally hurtful people. You're having a reaction right now, an impulse. You aren't thinking critically just yet. Remember that most people are just trying to do the best job they can, and the chances are that this individual is not trying to insult you.

Creating her own design is not necessarily an evil act. In fact, in most of the situations I've encountered this scenario or observed other designers come up against it, it's merely due to the individual finding it difficult to articulate everything she wanted to say about the design and thinking it would be easier if she tried to show you.

Hmm... *"Show me. Don't tell me."* Who does that sound like?

Correct me if I'm wrong, but hasn't the design community *en masse* used that as a kind of mantra to describe the inefficiencies we often encounter when trying to verbally describe things?

Similarly, getting a list of changes back as feedback might just mean that the individual has jumped to identifying solutions to the challenges she perceives rather than articulating those challenges back to you as feedback.

Of course, there is the possibility that the thinking behind the changes the individual is proposing might be personally motivated. The next steps in this process will work toward helping you identify if that is the case. Even if it is, it can be worth working to understand what this person is telling you, because you never know where a valuable insight might come from.

Step 2: Take note

Although she most likely isn't trying to play the role of your archnemesis, this does give you some insight into what your engagement might be like if you continue to work with this individual, and in many cases, you'll have to.

It isn't a bad thing. Good collaboration is rarely a natural occurrence. It takes deliberate action and consideration from the people involved. Getting a sense for how people share their thoughts and ideas can help you tailor how you work with them and increase the efficiency of your communications and idea-sharing back and forth.

Moreover, in the off chance that you're working with Satan himself, this might be one of your first signs...

Step 3: Critique the directive feedback

On your own, compare the contents and elements of the person's work or recommended changes and ask yourself the following:

- How does his design differ from yours? What specific changes is he proposing?

- Why might he be proposing these changes? What is he trying to achieve? What problems is he trying to solve and how is he trying to solve them?

- Did you try to solve for those same problems in your design? How? How does your solution differ from his?

- If you didn't try to solve for some of those same objectives, why not? Was it a deliberate omission on your part? An oversight?

- Looking at his proposed changes, what aspects of the design and its elements might he be indicating are of primary importance to him?

Make notes as you ask yourself these questions. But again, keep the notes to yourself. By doing this, you give yourself some time to step back and think objectively about what the individual might be trying to tell you.

Step 4: Critique together

Set up some time with the person who has sent you directive feedback to discuss the designs or list of changes. Thank her for her feedback and let her know that in order to refine the design you'd like to discuss some questions with her regarding the thinking behind the choices he made.

In your discussion ask about the differences you noticed between your design and her proposed changes and ask why he made or is recommending the change. Again, what problems is he trying to solve? What was it about your design that she doesn't think is sufficient to solve that same problem? If the solutions she's designed are problematic in some way to the design or product—perhaps because they go against best practices or research—ask her about it.

Also, ask specifically about the things she isn't recommending be changed or similarities between her design and yours. Why are they there? Did she keep them for the same reasons you made them?

Now, because you're going to be trying to facilitate this discussion as a critique, you want to make use of any tools you have that will help. Earlier in the project, did you establish agreed-upon personas and scenarios? How about goals and design principles? (*Are you all sick of us mentioning these yet?*)

If you did, have them at the ready. These are the perfect foundation for your discussion. Instead of just comparing the two designs to each other, or your design with the critic's list of changes, you can compare them in regard to all of the things that the team had previously agreed were important to the success of the product.

This helps remove some of the my-idea-versus-your-idea atmosphere that might be present and helps focus the conversation on what the right decisions are for the success of the product.

If you don't have these tools, this might be your opportunity to begin to generate some. As you discuss why he made decisions and learn about the aspects of the solution that are most important to him and his vision, you can talk about how this compares with the findings of any research that's been done, and possibly, on-the-fly generate some principles and goals that you can use to help focus discussions as the project moves forward.

Now, maybe your project does have goals and principles defined, but as you're going through the critique you're finding that they really aren't helping. This can be a sign that the goals and principles you set are too broad. Remember, when asking whether design options adhere to a principle, more often the answer should be "no." If your principles and goals are too broad, this can be your chance to refine them through your discussion.

Goals should be connected to something measurable. If during the conversation you find in trying to critique against a particular goal that you have no way to meaningfully measure something to determine if the goal has been achieved or not, you might need to refine your goal.

In the course of your conversation, your goal is to essentially construct a critique of your original proposed design using your critic's design or changes as a discussion tool. You should be able to learn which design decisions you made that don't quite work well enough to meet desired objectives and aspects that are important to the product and the client as well as how they aren't working. You also should have an under-standing of the design decisions that are working.

Beyond that, if the individual you're working with is a teammate, stake-holder, or client, you should also be looking to come away with a bet-ter understanding of her vision and thoughts on how specific design challenges might be solved. Using that knowledge, you can incorpo-rate elements of her solutions into a revised design where they work and fit best without compromising the integrity of the creation just so that people have something to point to and say, "I came up with that." Remember, a good idea can come from anywhere.

Step 5: Move forward together

Armed with a better understanding of your original proposed design you should now be able to iterate upon it in a way that strengthens its alignment with your research, design principles, and so on.

Of course, you have the option of ending your discussion by sitting down at your desk, making your revisions, and sending your updated design back out for feedback. But think about it for a second, and make sure that ending the discussion is the right thing to do at this time.

In most of the situations we've seen where this comes up, particularly when collecting feedback from teammates, stakeholders, or clients (as opposed to outside individuals), this approach is repeatedly problematic because it's exactly what caused the issue in the first place. The designer or team came up with their proposal and sent it over in an email with a few sparse instructions on how the client, stakeholder, and others should send back their thoughts.

You've got some opportunities here.

One possibility is for you to set up some time with the individual(s) and explore some of the changes together. Work together to generate multiple possibilities for a change and then refine them collaboratively. This gives you more insight into their thinking and gives you more opportunities to help them understand the design process.

Another thing to think about is how you'll collect feedback throughout the rest of the project. Not everything can be done together in real time. There will be times when you need to put something together and then get other people's thoughts in order to make changes. We've always found it's best to collect feedback in person (physically or remotely), because then we're able to structure and facilitate the conversation around critique.

For the situations in which someone proposes a change, we're immediately able to ask her why and get a better understanding of what it is she's trying to do. Yes, there are times when schedules are tight and we can't talk about everything we need to on our call, but by beginning the discussion in this way, we find that the remaining feedback that is sent by email is often much more useful than if all we'd done to initiate things was send her an email with our design and a request for her feedback.

If the individual is a member of your project, moving forward, consider reaching out to her a little earlier in the process. Share design concepts with her and, if appropriate, ensure that she is invited to team critiques. Be transparent with your design process and what you are trying to accomplish with your designs. Keep an open dialogue with the person.

Hopefully this will help the individual feel more comfortable communicating about designs with you and lead to more productive conversations and less bulleted lists or designs in response to your designs.

Central Idea

When situations become challenging, try to steer the conversation back to the main concerns. Engage the person or participants with whom you are working by keeping the conversation centered on the product.

Wrapping Up

Any time that we are collaborating with others, there are bound to be communication miscues, conflict, and frustration. This is the nature of working with people.

We are all different with differing personalities, character traits, and ideas as to how things should work. We should expect that there will be some level of communication gaps and even conflict, but by no means does this mean that we should enter working relationships looking to be combative.

Instead, we should be aware of the possible causes for these challenges and arm ourselves with tactics, a bit of extra patience, and a resolve to keep things focused on the project and its objectives, even if they begin to feel personal.

In this chapter, we covered different situations that you might encounter. Here are some of the key takeaways:

- Not all feedback is wanted, relevant, or actionable. This is to be expected and we should do our best to salvage what we can from it, if possible.

- When giving feedback to someone who has difficulty receiving it, be considerate, focus your language on the work (not the person) and the iterative aspect of critique, be honest, and balance the conversation around strengths and weakness.

- Facilitating reactive or directive feedback relies heavily on a methodical asking of the question "Why?"

- Ensuring that everyone involved in a group critique has an understanding of what useful feedback (critique) is and what the focus of the conversation should be on can go a long way toward keeping conversations efficient as well as providing tools to refocus them when they go astray.

- If someone has responded to proposed designs by sending her own versions of the design, take a step back and look at what she sent, analyze the differences between the proposed design and hers, and then follow up to discuss it with her.

- Use preestablished artifacts such as goals, personas, scenarios, and principles to center conversations.

- If you know someone is going to be difficult or tends to be difficult in meetings, communicate with that person ahead of time.

Communication is at the core of critique. When things start to go awry, the best way to get things back on track is to refocus the conversations on the objectives. Putting the focus back on the product can get to the intent of unwanted critique or situations in which someone is being difficult.

[7]

Summary: Critique Is at the Core of Great Collaboration

We have covered many concepts discussing how to critique and improve the conversations surrounding design. Some of the content might have resonated with you, whereas other parts might seem interesting but a bit difficult to make use of with your teams. This is OK. Although there are a lot of similarities in how we work with companies, teams, and clients, there is no rubber-stamp solution to improving design conversations that will work for everyone.

Critique is not just for designers. It is not owned by design; it's for anyone looking to improve whatever it is that they are developing. Though we mention design and designers a lot throughout the book, the thoughts and concepts shared in this book are equally of value to product owners, project managers, developers, and basically anyone who is working with others to create something.

Moving Beyond Feedback

Feedback is an important part of the design process; it is crucial that we move past the general understanding that many of us have of feedback, and build a shared understanding with our teams of what it means to the design process and how it should be used. When we begin doing this with our teams, we will begin to improve our conversations surrounding designs, which in turn leads to better collaboration.

Feedback has three main forms: direction, reaction, and critique. Direction and reaction do not help us better understand the effectiveness of aspects and elements of the design. Critique is a form of feedback by which we analyze a design against the objectives we have for it through critical thinking.

Having a more detailed understanding of feedback and how critique can benefit our teams has the ability to impact so many facets of our design process. As we embrace the use of critique, we begin to build a shared vocabulary around the products we are designing, making communication, collaboration, and consensus more attainable. Iteration on our products also becomes more effective as these other areas improve.

Understanding feedback is only the beginning; we also need to know how to apply feedback in conversations with those with whom we're working. Observe the people, personalities, and structures of the teams and clients you work with to uncover what you can do to help improve your critiques and design conversations in the contexts in which you work.

As we work to understand how to best approach feedback with our teams, it is important that intent be the foundational component of critique. Intent can be self-focused, based on ulterior motives or personal agendas, or it can be product-focused, where the choices we make are based on what is best for the product.

Adopting Critique

These two forms of intent affect both the giving and receiving of feedback, and if intent is wrong on either side it can really throw a wrench into the works. If we can keep the focus on the product, we have a much better chance at collaborating better. One way we can do this is by using the framework and best practices we shared in Chapter 2.

By asking the questions in the framework, we are using critical thinking to understand how to give helpful feedback to others. Leading with questions helps not only show interest in someone else's process, but it also helps to instigate a dialogue, which is really what critique is.

UNDERSTANDING THE ORGANIZATIONAL CULTURE

Understanding the culture you work in is a big part of improving critique and collaboration. Look at the culture in which you are working and note the areas where you think the culture will support efforts for improved communication and collaboration. Look also to the areas that are going to need some work. It is important to set realistic expectations about what you want to change for the better. Going in with guns blazing and no intent on being flexible probably won't get you very far.

But, if you go in with the intent to educate those you work with and are willing to find a common ground, you will begin to set the foundation for more productive conversations.

INTEGRATING CRITIQUE WITH YOUR PROCESS

Making critique a part of your process can have challenges and might not work as expected on your first try, but don't give up; continue to practice exchanging feedback and talking about your designs with your teams. Adam and I suggest using this book as a reference as you navigate the waters of discussing designs and solutions with others. As mentioned in previous chapters, the more you critique the more you will become comfortable with talking about your work with others and receiving feedback on it. It can be intimidating when you first start out. Trust me, we have shared in that feeling and still do at times. Don't be held back by believing you must be an expert right from the outset. It is a living process and as you do it more, you have the chance to improve how you (and your team) critique, see what works for you, what doesn't, and make adjustments.

Start small, observe those you work with and see who among them would be open to talking about critique, and invite them to a casual conversation. Choose a simple setting such as lunch or coffee to open up the discussion and see if you can set a regular time to meet, or if they are open to something more spontaneous as the opportunities arise. The more you do this, the more comfortable you will become talking about your designs with others. You will also become more comfortable with the process of critique and using the techniques we have shared in this book. The more you get used to talking about your designs in the context of critique, invite others to participate, and educate them about the value of critique, collaboration, and improved communication.

FACILITATING CRITIQUE

As you work on your critique skills, it is also crucial that you make sure to practice facilitating critique. Facilitation is a big part of the critique process, serving as a guide, keeping things on track, and making it easier to gather and record feedback. Try different approaches, whether it is using a round-robin technique to ensure that everyone contributes, or quotas that help participants frame their feedback in a more understandable way for everyone.

Preparing for the sessions, and getting materials out to the team ahead of time also goes a long way; it helps set the expectations for team members and helps them to come prepared. Follow-up emails and conversations are great tools for maintaining the momentum with the team after a session. Facilitation provides the structure and framework needed to improve communication and collaboration.

Coping with Difficult Situations

The more you critique, the more likely it is that you will eventually encounter different situations that can be frustrating, whether it is difficult people or lack of facilitation in meetings. Remember, it's not about judgment; it's about improvement based on analysis. If there are questions or concerns about your work, don't worry; it is a part of the process, and the chances are that you are still an awesome human being. The more we keep this in mind and focus on what will help us to improve the product when receiving feedback, the easier these difficult situations will be to work through. Collaboration isn't always easy, but by improving how you handle feedback and communicate with others, you can better work through these frustrating situations and still derive value from them.

Conversations and the people with whom we engage in them can be complicated. When we understand this going into them, we can prepare ourselves with the tools and techniques to make the discussions less difficult and derive more value from them.

Keep in mind that how people respond to critique can have a lot to do with their personal experiences, lack of experience with it, and cultural upbringing. As you work with others, listen, observe, and try to understand where they are coming from and what is influencing how they interact in these settings. As you begin to understand the various influencers, reach out to individuals, explain the purpose and value of critique, and help them feel more comfortable with the process.

We are providing you with a cheat sheet (*http://www.discussingdesign.com/downloads/Critique_CheatSheet.pdf*) to have handy that summarizes many of the helpful points in this book at a glance. In the cheat sheet we outline important things to remember about giving and receiving feedback, tips and techniques for facilitating critique, dealing with difficult situations, and making critique a part of your process. Besides using this cheat sheet for your own reference, you might want to share it with your team as a tool to use in preparation for and during your critique sessions. The more you do to help your team understand critique and help team members understand how to participate in a productive way, the sooner you will begin to see improvements in your design conversations.

Dive In

All you need to do is begin, dive in, and have a conversation with someone on your team or with a peer. Try to use the techniques in this book, see how they help shape your conversations, and see how others respond to them. Share, educate, and continue to push for better feedback, even if it is just a little bit at a time. Critique is at the core of great collaboration, and great collaboration brings teams together to create great products. Go forth, create, critique, and collaborate.

The 10 Bad Habits That Hurt Critique

Introduction

Adam and I often are asked for tips on what can be done to avoid critique sessions becoming a train wreck. This book has covered a lot of tips and techniques for making your critiques more productive; we would like to pull out a few things to keep in mind when going into a critique. These are things that you can work on by yourself or with your team. As we have mentioned, critique takes repetition, practicing the positive things we can do as well as training to avoid the bad habits that can put hurdles in the way of good communication and positive critiques. We have identified 10 common bad habits that negatively affect our critiques; we will give a brief definition of each so that you can have them as a handy reference

REACTING

Reactions in and of themselves are not bad; we all have them. In the context of critique, when we mention reacting as a bad habit we are talking about a response that has not been thought through to what we are seeing or hearing when someone presents a design. When we verbalize or act on our initial reactions without taking time to better understand what we are responding to and why we are having the reaction we are, we put ourselves in a position to provide information that isn't helpful to the presenter.

Instead of just reacting with the first thought that comes to mind (it doesn't matter whether it is accurate), hold on to that thought and think about some questions that will help you understand what you are seeing and hearing better.

What are the objectives of the design? What elements relate to those objectives? Are they successful? Why or why not? These are all questions to think through either on your own or with the person sharing her work. You can use the answers that you receive to compare against your initial reaction, and then you will find yourself in a place to offer informed, helpful feedback, or to keep your initial reaction to yourself.

BEING SELFISH

Giving critique isn't about telling someone what we would have created or manipulating situations to get our own way. And it's not about demonstrating to the group how smart we might be or how great our ideas are. Giving critique isn't about us at all.

But we often see individuals doing exactly these things. Offering feedback not on what has been designed, but instead commenting on what they think should have been done. This does little to help designers understand whether their designs will or won't be effective, and it does even less to keep a team collaborating smoothly.

GETTING DEFENSIVE

It can be very common to become defensive or protective over our work. Our work is our passion; our blood, sweat, and tears, laid out for oth¬ers to just pick apart, or at least it feels that way. By focusing on defending our work or worrying about what we think others will think of us if there are imperfections in our designs (which there always will be), we take the focus off the product and place it squarely on us. This is a self-focused approach to critique and to design.

Critique is not about personal judgment; it is about analysis and improvement. The success of the product we are building should be the main focus; this means we need to keep the focus on the product by being willing to look at our work objectively with our teams. Analyzing what is working and what isn't will help our team know what it needs to do to ensure that the product meets its goals.

Getting defensive over our work only puts hurdles in the way of com¬munication and collaboration. Explain your work, do not defend it. In a productive critique environment, our work is not under attack, it is being analyzed collectively so that the team and product can benefit from the insights provided.

Defending our designs can be a hard habit to get out of, but if we com¬mit to reminding ourselves that we are working together as a team to analyze and improve them, it makes it easier explain our design deci¬sions and gather feedback.

STARTING FROM DISPARATE FOUNDATIONS

Everyone comes into critique with their own sets of expertise, experience, and skills. This diversity in perspectives can be helpful as they can help provide us with diverse insights. We run into trouble when the core foundation underneath these expectations and ideas of what the product should accomplish are not aligned across team members and clients.

If we do not start from a common foundation of what objectives the product should be working toward, each individual might try to steer the product according to his or her own priorities. It would be like an Olympic rowing team trying to win a race while everyone in the boat is trying to row in their own direction. It's safe to say that their chances of success are limited.

For teams to have productive conversations and critiques, there needs to be a set of agreements that underpins their unique expertise and perspectives, a common understanding of the core goals to unite the team and center the conversations surrounding design.

When agreed upon by the team, items such as product goals, personas, scenarios, and principles are useful in setting a solid foundation for collaborative activities and critiques because they provide information about a desired future state and the guiderails a solution should work within to reach it.

LACKING FOCUS

If critiques lack focus, things can go off the rails quickly and make it difficult for the team to understand and gather useful insights. Critique, and more important, the participants in a critique, need structure to help keep the conversations focused and to help them understand the type of feedback they should be giving and how they should be sharing it.

By identifying the specifics that we want feedback on and making sure that the team understands them, we can avoid everyone just firing away feedback for any part of the design in any order they want.

Send out the plan for what you hope to accomplish during the critique and explain the structure that will allow the session to meet those goals. Share the work to be critiqued ahead of time as well as the type of feedback you are looking for so participants can come prepared.

If necessary, use basic facilitation techniques such as going around the room in a round-robin fashion to help keep things moving. Another useful technique is to use different lenses (ways and angles to look at things) to help draw out specific perspectives and insights.

FOCUSING ON WHAT ISN'T WORKING

So much of the time when thinking of critique, it can be easy to fall into the trap of only identifying what isn't working. This line of thinking does not capture the entire purpose of critique. Yes, we need to identify what isn't working so that we can improve upon it, but we also need to identify what is working to continue to pursue those solutions. If we see that a certain solution is working, we can possibly find use for it later in the project or on other projects because we know that it already works.

It is also important to find strengths in a design or solution so that there is balance in the critique; a good way to do this is by providing a structure for participants to use when giving feedback. An example of this would be asking each participant to identify two things they think are working in the solution and two things that cause concern.

LACK OF DISCUSSION

Critique is a dialog, an exploration and analysis of the solutions we are proposing for a certain set of problems. Critique is not a list of revisions to be carried out like a short-order cook.

To truly find out if a design or solution is on the right path, it is crucial for teams to talk about why something might or might not be working. If critique is a dialogue, this means that those giving and receiving critique need to be able to measure solutions against goals, share insights, and ask questions to ensure understanding. You can't achieve this type of dialog by a to-do list sent in an email or over chat. We need to discuss our designs.

AVOIDING PARTICIPATION

If we want to open up the dialogue during a critique and help ensure that we are getting productive participation from others, we should make sure that we are critiquing our work alongside them.

When we step around to the other side of the table (figuratively speaking) and start critiquing with the rest of the team, we begin to break down the me-versus-you mentality that can often happen during a critique and make everyone more comfortable with the conversation.

We have seen that actively critiquing our own work with the rest of the team can help them feel more comfortable with providing feedback; they are less worried about offending because you are critiquing with them.

PROBLEM SOLVING

Critique is a form of analysis. When we are participating in a critique, we are analyzing our solutions based on what we collectively understand the goals of the product to be. When we switch from analysis to problem solving, we are switching from one type of brain function to another.

Doing so, especially when a group of people is involved, can cause disruption to the discussion. Some individuals are still analyzing the original design, some are trying to understand or analyze then new ideas being discussed, and others may be trying to formulate their own solutions.

By keeping our critiques focused on analyzing the design at hand, we facilitate a better, more complete discussion. After wich we can work to explore potential solutions to address any weaknesses or opportunities raised during the critique.

CONFUSING CRITIQUE WITH REVIEW

Many of us have spent time in design reviews, and they are often considered the same as critique. Reviews are not critique. Design reviews are often scheduled to get some sort of approval to move forward or go live. Most of the attendees in a design review (and there are usually far too many for productive conversations) are there to ensure that the part of the design they own gains approval and moves into the final product, and most of the decisions and approvals are tied to deadlines. This type of environment is not conducive to productive critiques.

Do not rely on design reviews for critique. You should critique leading up to the design review so that there are no surprises and so that your design reviews go smoothly.

[*Index*]

divergent thinking activities, 95–97
document cameras, 72
documenting open questions, 137

E

early critique, 85–86
ecosystems, designing products within, 51
email
    critique notifications by, 119–120
    real conversations and, 43
emotional goals, 62
equality rule (critique), 111–112
Erb, Veronica, 73
evaluation criteria, sharing, 61
everyone is a critic rule (critique), 112
everyone is equal rule (critique), 111–112
expectations, setting (sessions), 145

F

facade of authority, 125–126
Facebook, bad critiques on, 23
facilitating critique
    collection/follow up, 136–139
    defining scope and goals, 126–127
    designer presence, 135–136
    direct inquiry, 131–132
    facade of authority, 125–126
    implementing active listening, 128–130
    overview, 109–110
    practicing, 171–172
    preparation/kick-off, 117–124
    Round Robin and quotas, 130–131
    rules of critique, 111–116
    taking notes, 133
    Thinking Hats technique, 132–133
    third-party facilitators, 134–135
feedback
    avoiding, 38
    culturally acceptable, 6
    direction-based, 7–8
    directive, 162–167
    forms of, 169
    incomplete, 24–25
    not listening to, 37
    online tools for, 44
    overview, ix–x

positive, 29, 161
preferential, 25
problems with in design reviews, 105–106
reactive, 118, 158–161
requesting, 2–4
requesting specifics, 44
sandwich method, 153–154
seeking validation via, 38–39
selfish, 23–24
tactfully inviting, 28–29
types of, 5–8
understanding and applying, 169–170
unsolicited, 155–158
untimely, 24
using "five whys" to get, 148
filtering reactions (giving critique), 27
findings, reviewing critique, 137–138
"Five Whys" to get feedback, 148
focus
    lacking (bad habits), 177–178
    on what isn't working (bad habits), 178
formal critique, 82–83
foundations
    for critique, setting, 56–66
    starting from disparate (bad habits), 177
frankensteining, 12

G

giver role in critique, 21–22
giving critique
    bad critique characteristics, 22–24
    best practices for, 25–29
    framework for, 33–35
    giving bad critique, 22–24
    identifying objectives/choices, 34
    intent of, 21–22
    overview, 22
    questions for evaluating design objectives, 34
    respectful questions to ask, 32–33
    Zappos website example, 31–32
goals
    and scope of sessions, defining, 126–127
    emotional, 62
    overview of, 63–64

About the Authors

 **Aaron Irizarry**, known in luchadore circles as El Cubano Magnifico, is Director of User Experience for Nasdaq Product Design and has been building online products for startups and large corporations for over 10 years. Aaron is also a public speaker and consults with companies providing design studio and collaborative critique workshops to help their product teams and stakeholders/managers improve the discussion around product design.

 **Adam Connor**, most recognizable by his magnificent beard, is an Experience Designer and VP of Organizational Design at Mad*Pow, a design agency based in Portsmouth, NH. Since 2009, he has been helping teams and organizations all over the world understand how to better collaborate to create innovative new products and services. His work at Mad*Pow and extensive background in experience design, computer science, illustration, and film has taught him the value of delivering and receiving constructive feedback in the design process and the role it plays in enabling teams to work together creatively and productively.

Have it your way.

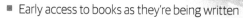

Get even more for your money.

Join the O'Reilly Community, and register the O'Reilly books you own. It's free, and you'll get:

- $4.99 ebook upgrade offer
- 40% upgrade offer on O'Reilly print books
- Membership discounts on books and events
- Free lifetime updates to ebooks and videos
- Multiple ebook formats, DRM FREE
- Participation in the O'Reilly community
- Newsletters
- Account management
- 100% Satisfaction Guarantee

Signing up is easy:

1. Go to: oreilly.com/go/register
2. Create an O'Reilly login.
3. Provide your address.
4. Register your books.

Note: English-language books only

To order books online:
oreilly.com/store

For questions about products or an order:
orders@oreilly.com

To sign up to get topic-specific email announcements and/or news about upcoming books, conferences, special offers, and new technologies:
elists@oreilly.com

For technical questions about book content:
booktech@oreilly.com

To submit new book proposals to our editors:
proposals@oreilly.com

O'Reilly books are available in multiple DRM-free ebook formats. For more information:
oreilly.com/ebooks

Milton Keynes UK
Ingram Content Group UK Ltd.
UKHW021533201123
432922UK00003B/6